Christmas 2011

Dearest Keira,
    For your inspiration & enjoyment,
      With love,
        Mom

ARCHITECTS OF THE WORLD

Whitney

Tadao Ando • Baumschlager & Eberle • Günter Behnisch • William Bruder • Santiago Calatrava • Coop Himmelb(l)au • Wolfgang Döring • Carles Ferrater • Norman Foster • Frank O. Gehry • Peter Gluck • Michael Graves • Heikkinen & Komonen • Herzog & de Meuron • Steven Holl • Arata Isozaki • Toyo Ito • Helmut Jahn • Jourda & Perraudin • Rem Koolhaas • Kengo Kuma • Kisho Kurokawa • Ricardo Legorreta • Mark Mack • Fumihiko Maki • Mecanoo • Richard Meier • Enric Miralles • Rafael Moneo • Morphosis • Hiroshi Nakao • Eric Owen Moss • Nikken Sekkei • Jean Nouvel • Cesar Pelli • Dominique Perrault • Renzo Piano • Gabriel Poole • Antoine Predock • Kazuyo Sejima • Alvaro Siza • Naoyuki Shirakawa • Eduardo Souto de Moura • Ben van Berkel • Erick van Egeraat • von Gerkan + Marg • Wolfgang Döring • Carles Ferrater • Norman Foster • Frank O. Gehry • Peter Gluck • Michael Graves • Heikkinen & Komonen • Herzog & de Meuron • Steven Holl • Arata Isozaki • Toyo Ito • Helmut Jahn • Jourda & Perraudin • Rem Koolhaas • Kengo Kuma • Kisho Kurokawa • Ricardo Legorreta • Mark Mack • Fumihiko Maki • Mecanoo • Richard Meier • Enric Miralles • Rafael Moneo • Morphosis • Hiroshi Nakao • Eric Owen Moss • Nikken Sekkei • Jean Nouvel • Cesar Pelli • Dominique Perrault • Renzo Piano • Gabriel Poole • Antoine Predock • Kazuyo Sejima • Alvaro Siza • Naoyuki Shirakawa • Eduardo Souto de Moura • Ben van Berkel • Erick Van Egeraat • von Gerkan + Marg •

ARCHITECTS OF THE WORLD

Author	Francisco Asensio Cerver
Editorial Manager	Paco Asensio
Project coordinator	Ivan Bercedo (architect)
Design & layout	Mireia Casanovas Soley
Text	
Ivan Bercedo	Tadao Ando, Baumschlager & Eberle, Günter Behnisch, William Bruder, Santiago Calatrava, Coop Himmelb(l)au, Carles Ferrater, Norman Foster, Frank O. Gehry, Michael Graves, Herzog & de Meuron, Steven Holl, Arata Isozaki, Toyo Ito, Rem Koolhaas, Kengo Kuma, Kisho Kurokawa, Ricardo Legorreta, Fumihiko Maki, Richard Meier, Enric Miralles, Rafael Moneo, Hiroshi Nakao, Nikken Sekkei, Jean Nouvel, Renzo Piano, Gabriel Poole, Kazuyo Sejima, Naoyuki Shirakawa, Eduardo Souto de Moura
Marta Thorres	Wolfgang Döring, Peter Gluck, Heikkinen & Komonen, Helmut Jahn, Jourda & Perraudin, Mark Mack, Mecanoo, Morphosis, Eric O. Moss, Cesar Pelli, Dominique Perrault, Antoine Predock, Alvaro Siza, Ben van Berkel, Erick van Egeraat, von Gerkan + Marg
Translation	Elaine Fradley
Copy editing	Viviane Vives
Proofreading	David Buss

© 1998 Francisco Asensio Cerver

Published by
Whitney Library of Design
An imprint of Watson & Guptill Publications
New York

ISBN: 0-8230-0287-X

Printed in Spain
Gràfiques Ibèria s.a.

No part of this publication may be reproduced, stored in a retrieval system or transmitted in any form or by means, electronic, mechanical, photocopying, recording or otherwise, without the prior written permission of the owner of the copyright.

8	Tadao Ando
12	Baumschlager & Eberle
16	Günter Behnisch
20	William Bruder
24	Santiago Calatrava
28	Coop Himmelb(l)au
32	Wolfgang Döring
36	Carles Ferrater
40	Norman Foster
44	Frank O. Gehry
48	Peter Gluck
52	Michael Graves
56	Heikkinen & Komonen
60	Herzog & de Meuron
64	Steven Holl
68	Arata Isozaki
72	Toyo Ito
76	Helmut Jahn
80	Jourda & Perraudin
84	Rem Koolhaas
88	Kengo Kuma
92	Kisho Kurokawa
96	Ricardo Legorreta
100	Mark Mack
104	Fumihiko Maki
108	Mecanoo
112	Richard Meier
116	Enric Miralles
120	Rafael Moneo
124	Morphosis
128	Hiroshi Nakao
132	Eric Owen Moss
136	Nikken Sekkei
140	Jean Nouvel
144	Cesar Pelli
148	Dominique Perrault
152	Renzo Piano
156	Gabriel Poole
160	Antoine Predock
164	Kazuyo Sejima
168	Naoyuki Shirakawa
172	Alvaro Siza
176	Eduardo Souto de Moura
180	Ben van Berkel
184	Erick van Egeraat
188	von Gerkan + Marg

The Bible story which exemplifies the union of different peoples is the one that tells us about the Tower of Babel. A work of architecture is a joint project if ever there was one. Every individual work is the result of the collaboration of workers, craftsmen and experts, and it is hard to pinpoint the ultimate contribution of each one to the finished product. This makes it clearly unjust to assign a project to just one author, as though it were a novel, a painting or a sculpture. In this respect, architecture is more like the cinema, the theater or dance. Architects need to be surrounded by a group of people for their work to be made reality, and to a large extent the final result of the initial ideas produced by the architects depends not just on their own merit, but on collective know-how.

Even in their studios, architects rarely work alone; although they tend to work under the name of a single person, most studios involve a variable number of designers and architects who work in association with the main architect. In Europe today there are still many small studios (with fewer than 30 members), but in Asia and the USA most projects are managed by major firms which can have as many as a thousand workers.

Yet when we see a building by Richard Meier, Frank Gehry or Rem Koolhaas, although we know that hundreds of people have taken part in creating it, what stands out most of all is the personal stamp that Meier, Gehry or Koolhaas leave on their works. In this sense, even if we see architecture as a collective activity, it is always extremely interesting to analyze the individual vision of each architect. The pages that follow present some of the most outstanding buildings of recent years from the point of view of the architect. Most art museums and specialized journals present a work in isolation from the author's career, with no explanation of the motivations and particular interests which lie behind it (which makes it practically impossible for the novice to decipher); here, however, we have endeavored to show the latest projects of the various architects, placing them in the context of their careers as a whole.

Tadao Ando

1. Kidosaki House
1986

2. Vitra Conference Center
1993

Chikatsu-Asuka History Museum 1994

The remarkable coherence of Ando's work lies in its solid intellectual and theoretical grounding. His architecture has a will for poetry and ontology, being designed as the transference of man's two dimensions: space and time. For Ando, the role of architecture is to build a place able to hold time. And time comes into being in two ways: one objective, the other subjective; objectively, in the changes associated with nature, the variations of light and shadow during the day, one season giving way to the next; and subjectively, in man's perception, subject to movement and memory.

The bare, austere spaces of his buildings are designed to record the parallel course of shadows and visitors. The constructed building is just one part of the work, allowing it to start and move in time. The work is the total sum of what is lasting, of what happens, and what man perceives. "The architecture which acquires quietude and balance through geometric order achieves dynamism thanks to natural phenomena and human movement," writes Tadao Ando in his article "Light, Shadow and Form" (Via 11, 1990)

Tadao Ando (Osaka, 1941), ex-boxer and self-taught architect, decided to devote himself to architecture almost by chance after buying a book about Le Corbusier. In the sixties, he traveled around America and Europe. His earliest work consisted mainly of family houses Azuma House (1975), Koshino House (1981), Kidosaki House (1986), etc. In the eighties, he designed a series of temples of extraordinarily ascetic and mystical beauty: the Mount Rokko Church (Kobe, 1986), the Chapel of Water (Hokkaido, 1988), the Chapel of Light (Osaka, 1989), and the Buddhist Temple (Hyogo, 1991).

International recognition has brought him major commissions, such as the remodeling of the Island of Nakanoshima, the Japanese Pavilion at Expo'92, the main offices of Benetton in Treviso, and a long list of museums built during the nineties. While in his family houses, small temples, and sanctuaries Ando achieves an extraordinary solemnity and spiritual force rare in modern architecture, in his large-scale public works, mysticism tends to be transformed into monumentality.

Chikatsu-Asuka History Museum

- Location: Minami-Kawachi, Osaka, Japan.
- Construction: 1994.
- Architect: Tadao Ando.
- Photographs: Shigeo Ogawa.

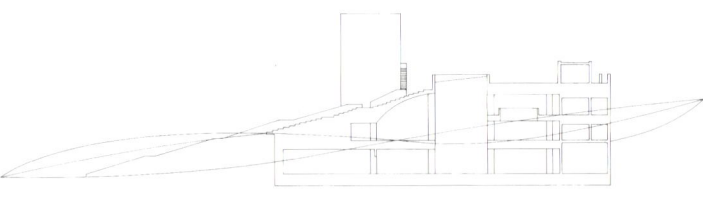 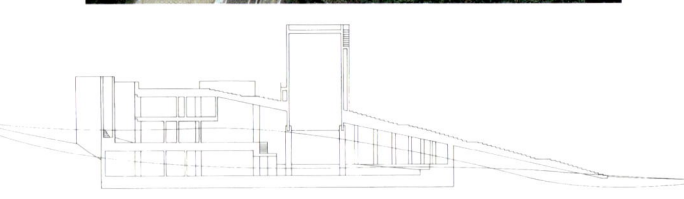

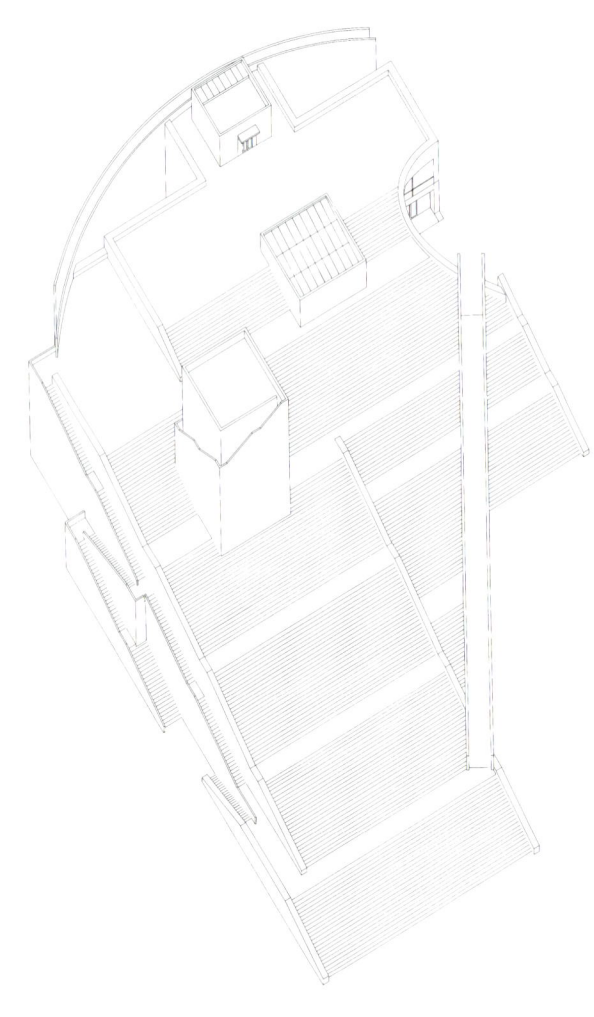

10 *Tadao Ando*

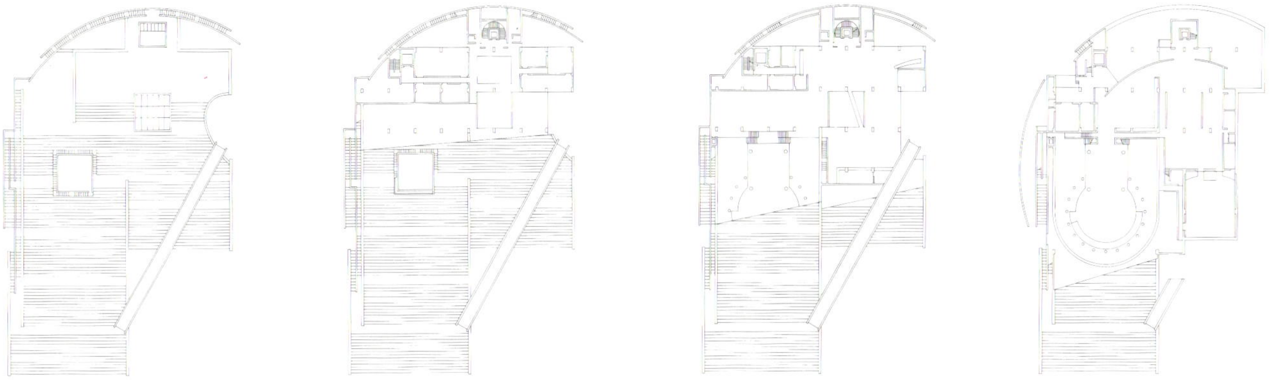

Chikatsu-Asuka History Museum is intended to disseminate and study the culture of the kofun. To integrate the museum with the tumuli, I designed it as a terraced hill which provides visitors with a panoramic view of the necropolis. Plum trees, a lake, and paths sprawling over the surrounding hills introduce the museum into the landscape and encourage outdoor activities. The roof is a great terraced plaza which can be used for theater productions, music festivals, and performances.
Inside the building, the exhibition areas are dark and the objects are displayed just as they were discovered in the tombs. Visitors feel as though they have entered a tomb and become immersed in time past. (Tadao Ando)

Chikatsu-Asuka History Museum

1. Burger House
1993

2. Lagertechnik
1994

3. Holz Altenried
1995

*Häusler House
1995*

Karl Baumschlager and Dietmar Eberle are part of an extraordinary generation of Austrian and Swiss architects (Herzog & de Meuron, Burkhalter & Sumi, Gigon & Guyer, Adolf Krischanitz, Roger Diener, etc.), characterized by an architecture that combines concise, simple geometric forms with careful treatment of the skin of buildings. Their buildings are conceived as geometric compositions immersed in the landscape. It is difficult to make out windows, balconies, or awnings in the traditional sense of the words. All these elements are reinterpreted by a rigorous geometry which dilutes them into the compact form of the building.

Under the influence of American minimalist sculptors (Judd, Andre, Morris, etc.) and parallel European trends, particularly Beuys, their architecture picks up the idea of an object set down in the landscape. Their work is the very opposite of organicism and, of course, picturesque naturalism: it is the product of the relationship between the building and its setting, despite its apparent hermeticism and spartan simplicity. The relationship with the landscape is established from the point of view of an intruder who has just arrived and is silently observing. Their architecture is intended as a reflective interlude rather than a continuance of the landscape.

Karl Baumschlager (Bregenz, 1956) studied at the Hochschule fur Angewandte Kunst in Vienna, where he studied under H. Hollein, W. Hozbauer, and O.M. Ungers, and graduated in 1982. Dietmar Eberle (Hittisau, 1952) studied at Vienna's Technical School and has lectured in Hanover, Vienna, and Zurich since 1982. The two set up their architecture studio in 1984. Their works in the nineties such as the Fischer School (Oberôsterreich, 1991), the Alcatel Headquarters (Lustenau, 1993), the Lagertechnik Offices (Wolfurt, 1994), the warehouse and showroom for Holz Alteried (Hergatz, 1995), the Martinspark Hotel (Dornbirn, 1995), and the remodeling of Raiffensen Bank (Bregenz, 1997) are all well known. Despite being a very young partnership, their body of work has become one of the most interesting in today's architecture scene in Europe.

Häusler House

- **Location:** Hard, Austria.
- **Construction:** 1995.
- **Architects:** Baumschlager & Eberle.
- **Associates:** Rainer Huchler; Ernst Mader (structures).
- **Photographs:** Eduard Hueber.

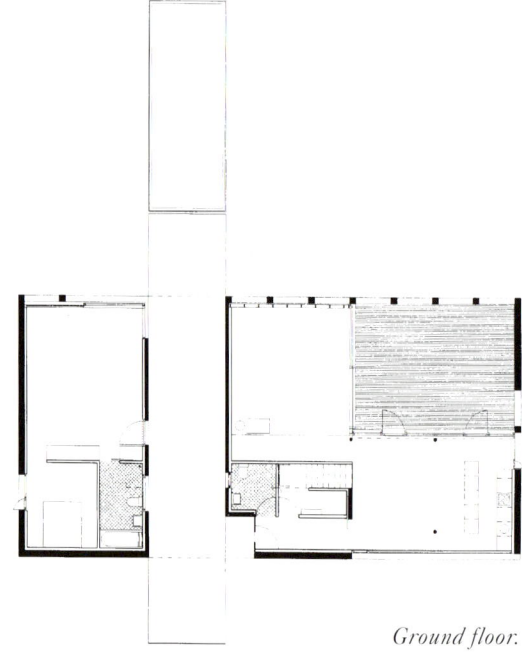

Ground floor.

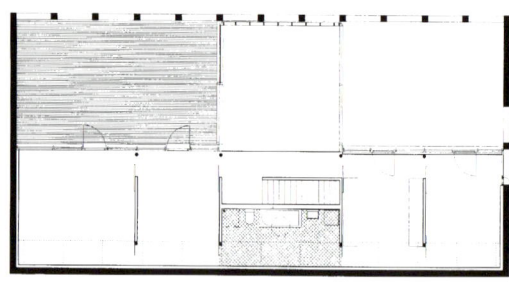

Second floor.

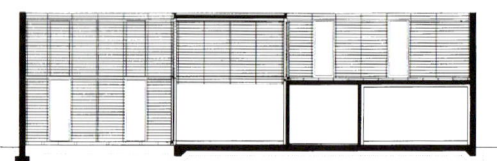

Longitudinal section.

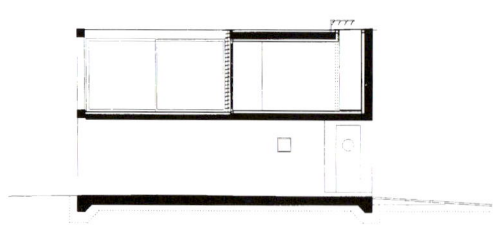

Transversal section.

14 *Baumschlager & Eberle*

Haüsler House has two skins, one in concrete and one in wood. A series of spaces, which function as inner courts, open up between the two. The house, designed by Baumschlager & Eberle, is consciously different from those around it; most of these are family houses built in a traditional architectural style with ridge roofs and no clear relationship between them or with the landscape.

Günter Behnisch

1. The Catholic Library of the University of Eichstatt
1988

2. Hysolar Institute
1987

3. Liginsland Kindergarten
1990

4. Charlotte House
1994

The Bundestag 1993

Behnisch's work represents the best sentiments to come out of Germany and Europe after the great tragedy of World War II. His buildings express profoundly democratic, social, and ecological convictions. His architecture is purposely anti-monumental and non-dramatic, endeavoring to respect nature and the spirit of place; the works shun abstract laws and absolute principles which, according to Behnisch, always do violence. Any type of relationship must be established on the basis of respect for what is particular and different. This is why his works often deploy the complexity inherent in a superposition of various systems and the development of greater freedom. This dispersion and blend of different materials gives increased depth to the final result.

He brings the same attitude to constructional details, and even to his drawings, as he does to the organization of his buildings. The imperfectly intersecting lines and the typed labeling carelessly-stuck to the plan are reflections of his open, tolerant approach.

Günter Behnisch (Dresden, 1922) studied at the Hochschule in Stuttgart, graduating in 1951. In 1952 he set up his own office, where he worked with Bruno Lambart until 1958 and, after 1966, with the architects F. Auer, W. Büxel, E. Tränkner, K. Weber, and M. Sabatke in the studio that became Behnisch & Partner, in 1979. Ever since he started working, Behnisch has developed an environmentally friendly architecture which calls for the use of new materials. The Ulm Engineering School (1958) was the first public building in Germany to be built entirely with prefabricated elements. The Munich Olympic Ring (1972), designed together with Otto Frei, is now one of the most interesting examples of the harmonious integration of high-tech infrastructures in a natural environment. Most of his projects are public buildings with a social function: kindergartens, schools, town halls, etc. He has also developed his relationship with architecture by teaching and getting involved in public institutions such as the Institute for Construction in Extreme Climates, the Schools Construction Institute, the German Research Association, etc.

■ The Bundestag

- ■ **Location:** Bonn, Germany.
- ■ **Construction:** 1993.
- ■ **Developer:** The Bundestag.
- ■ **Architects:** Günter Behnisch, Winfried Büxel, Manfred Sabatke, Erhard Tränkner.
- ■ **Associates:** Gerald Staib, Hubert Burkart, Eberhard Pritzer, Alexander von Salmuth, Ernst Tillmanns (project team).
- ■ **Photographs:** Behnisch & Partner, Christian Kandzia, Soene/Architekturphoto.

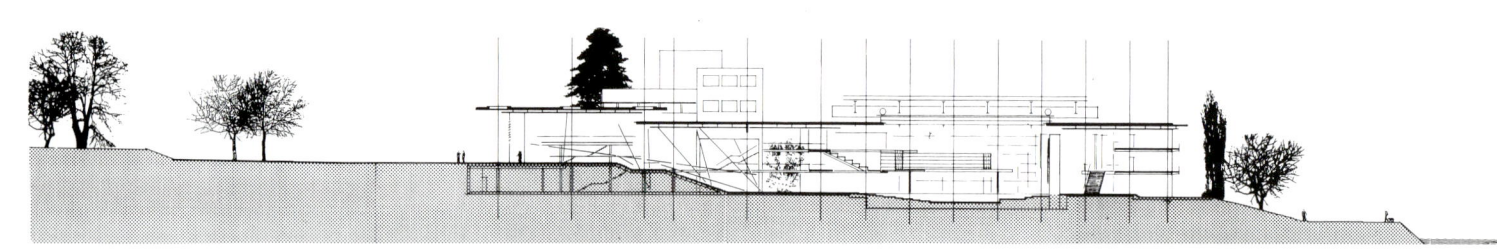

18 *Günter Behnisch*

The Parliament occupies a splendid location: close to the Rhine river and the long embankment promenade. Its considerable size called for particular care so as not to distort the landscape. The scale of the building is similar to that of the elements in the landscape. Behnisch plays on connections and cross-references between nature and architecture. The roof is practically transparent. Beneath the skylight, the hall becomes a small valley within a forest, where light shines in through the branches. Daytime and night, sunsets, seasons, winter snow, the leaden skies of autumn, colorful flowers in springtime: all of this is brought into the building. The decisions affecting the whole country take place in a very similar environment to the one where the people of the land we call Germany would have met two thousand years ago: a clearing in the woods.

The Bundestag 19

William P. Bruder

1. Kol-Ami Temple
   1994

2. Deer Valley Cave
   Art Museum
   1995

3. Riddell's
   1995

*Mad River Trips
1997*

The Arizona desert is one of few places left where architecture conserves an artistic, symbolic function, and is where William Bruder has been developing his body of work since the late seventies. His work picks up themes that Wright had approached in order to demonstrate a way of occupying the landscape by using place-specific materials, for greater visual integration into the desert; diluting the limits of the design. Bill Bruder's way of working produces projects that brim with unusual situations arising from his close contact with the work, and the fact that he handles the materials with his own hands. Bruder started out as a sculptor and has never lost his interest in the tangible.

Bruder's work unfolds an on-going dialogue with the landscape the hills, water, dryness, color and also with the vernacular architecture of Arizona: old rural buildings, mines, granaries, and so on. His buildings aim to evoke lyrical images of Arizona and, at the same time, to recover the simplest building materials by an exquisite re-use.

Bruder (Milwaukee, Wisconsin, 1946) studied sculpture at the University of Wisconsin, graduating in 1969. At the same time, he started working in collaboration with architecture studios and, as he himself explains, learnt from Goff how to listen to clients, from Soleri how to make something out of nothing, and from Schweikher the importance of rigor and attention to detail. The use of metaphor as an architectural resource is a strategy that William P. Bruder took from another great architect of the American desert: Antoine Predock.

In 1974, Bruder set up his own studio in Phoenix. During the nineties, his interest in architecture extended beyond the Arizona borders to the rest of the United States and the world. Some projects, such as Deer Valley Cave Art Museum (1994), Phoenix Central Library (1995), and Jackson Library in Wyoming (1996) have won many awards and the attention of international critics. Once again, we see how the most particular is not necessarily the most universal.

Mad River Trips

- Location: Jackson, Wyoming, USA.
- Construction: 1997.
- Architect: William P. Bruder.
- Associates: Wendell Burnette, Tim Christ, Jack De Bartolo III, Leah Schneider (design team).
- Photographs: Bill Timmerman.

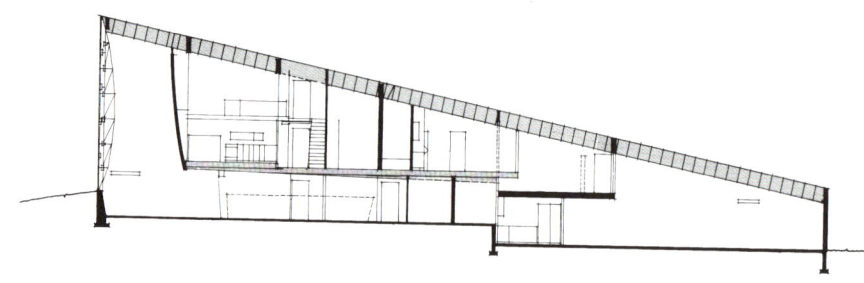

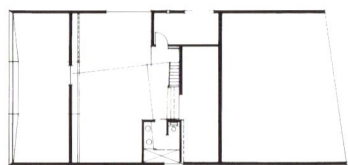

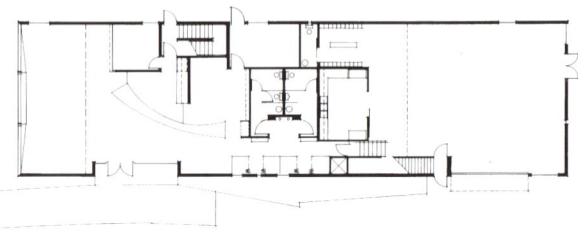

The building holds both the offices with warehouse and the home of the owners of this small firm which organizes rafting trips down the river.

22 *William Bruder*

Santiago Calatrava

1. Lucerne Station
1991

2. Montjuïc Communications Tower
1992

3. La Alameda Station Bridge
1994

4. Lyons-Satôlas Station
1995

*Footbridge in Bilbao
1997*

The work of Santiago Calatrava, architect and engineer, intuitively expresses the tensions that come together in what is static, unfolding the intrinsic poetry of the tectonic. His architecture is produced by stripping the idea right back, almost molding the form to capture its final movement.

But Calatrava's architecture not only represents gravitational tensions; it is also an exploration of the expressive potential of forces, it is the other side of the coin, the affirmation of a structural language which aims to be form and create text. For this reason, the technical solutions adopted by his buildings seem natural, despite being extremely sophisticated. This leads to their proximity to nature, to animal skeletons, and trees.

"My work is figurative rather than organic, in the sense that I am interested in certain sculptural-anatomical associations, based on tremendously purist static models. Working with isostatic structures almost inevitably leads you to natural schemes." (Santiago Calatrava)

As a child, Santiago Calatrava (Benimanet, 1951) attended an old arts and crafts school and even today, many years later, he continues to advocate learning directly from forms by drawing, alongside wood carvers, engravers, and glass workers.

Calatrava went on to qualify in Architecture from the University of Valencia and the ETH in Zurich. His multidisciplinary training, as architect and engineer, has allowed him to carry out a broad-based body of work, ranging from sculpture and furniture design to the construction of large-scale infrastructures.

His early works, dating from the late eighties—the Enrsting Factory, the Jakem Industrial Warehouse, Bärenmatte Concert Hall, Tabourettli Cabaret, and the roofs for the Canton School of Kawo Wohlen)—reveal structures very close to mechanics and movement.

His works in the nineties bring a sculptural approach to large-scale infrastructures—Barcelona's Communications Tower; bridges in Merida, Seville, Valencia, Bilbao; the remodeling of St. John the Divine in New York, the Kuwaiti Pavilion at Seville's Expo'92, and train stations in Zurich, Lyons and Lisbon, etc.

Footbridge in Bilbao

- Location: Bilbao, Spain.
- Construction: 1997.
- Architect: Santiago Calatrava.
- Client: City of Bilbao.
- Span: 210 ft.
- Photographs: Jordi Miralles.

The Uribitarte footbridge spans the 210 ft. of Bilbao's estuary. The structure of the tensed arch is steel, as are the ribs which support the totally glazed walkway. The metal structure is anchored to the ground by concrete elements which serve as ramps leading up to the level of the bridge.

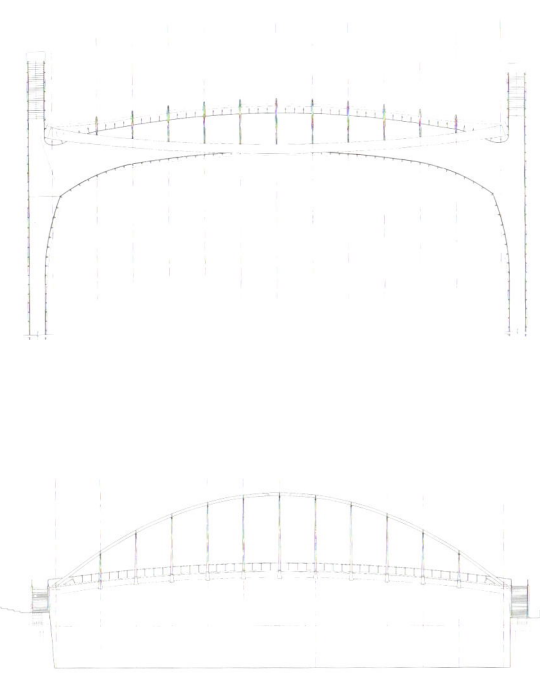
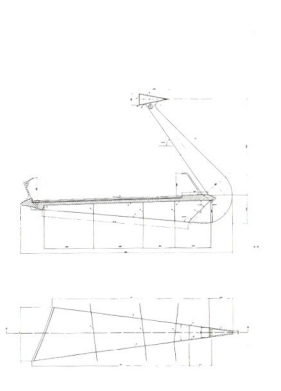
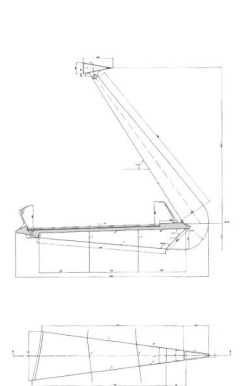
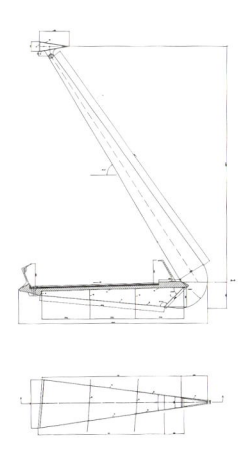
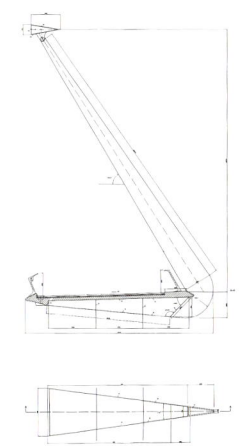

Footbridge in Bilbao

Coop Himmelb(l)au

1. Funder Werk 3 Factory
   1988-1989

2. Remodeling of a Penthouse flat in Vienna
                                        1990

3. Groningen Museum
   (Art Department)
   1994

28

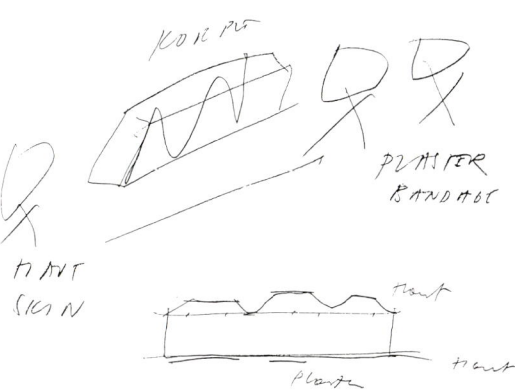

Seibersdorf Offices and Research Center 1995

The basis of Coop Himmelb(l)au's projects has always been a hasty yet intuitive drawing, produced after long talks about the possibilities and particular conditions of each specific case. The sketch is a way of pouring light on the project and drawing from subconscious strata. The drafts serve as a point of reference for the construction of a model, which is then introduced into the computer, with a coordinate associated to each point.

This strategy ensures that the project is not merely the product of a logical reasoning process; it also adopts an impulse, an energy and lines of force, with fractionated elements which produce surprise situations, interstices endowed with the value of the unusual. The anecdotal gives rise to situations which enrich the architecture, due to the multiplicity of sensations produced in this way. The project achieves unity by means of successive fragmentation, by breaking with planes and volume, in a series of asymmetrical situations.

Coop Himmelb(l)au, which literally means sky-blue cooperative, was set up in Vienna in 1968 by Wolf D. Prix (Vienna, 1942) and Helmut Swiczinsky (Poznan, 1944). Although Coop Himmelb(l)au's built work is not particularly extensive, its projects have received a great deal of attention, even if they were never actually built. They were included in the exhibition Deconstructivist Architecture organized by Philip Johnson at the New York MOMA, and the Center Georges Pompidou devoted a retrospective to them. The work of Coop Himmelb(l)au, along with that of the Americans Peter Eisenman and Daniel Libeskind, was one of the foremost references of deconstructivist thinking in the eighties and early nineties.

It is because we value the theoretical basis of their architecture that we consider it equally interesting to analyze their built constructions for themselves and not just as references of an intellectual trend. In this sense, the work of Coop Himmelb(l)au has the virtue of blazing trails and bringing hitherto unknown situations to architecture.

Seibersdorf Offices and Research Center

- **Location:** Seibersdorf, Austria.
- **Construction:** 1995.
- **Developer:** Austrian Research Center.
- **Architects:** Wolf D. Prix, Helmut Swiczinsky.
- **Associates:** Sam, Hopfner, Hornung, Mündl, Pillhofer, Spiess, Péan, Postl (design team).
- **Photographers:** Gerald Zugmann, Hélène Bisnet.

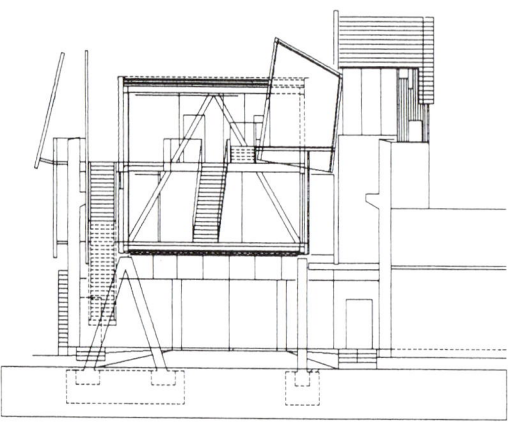

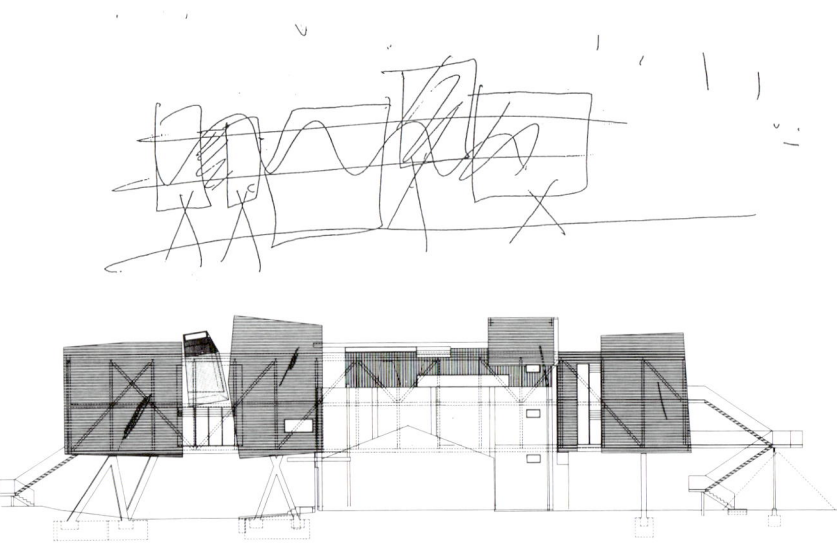

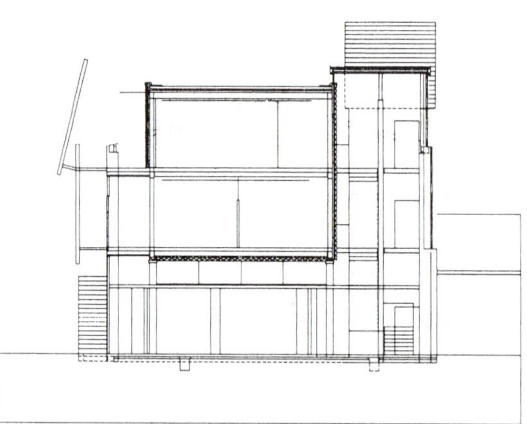

30 *Coop Himmelb(l)au*

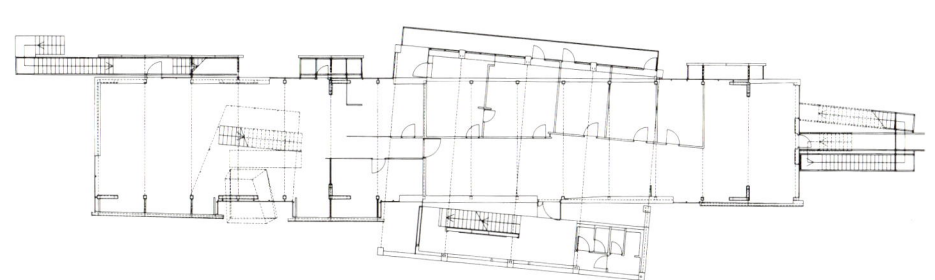

This volume, which has been added onto the existing one, is laid out over two floors and supported by a series of sloping columns, some of which are laid out in a cross shape. Rather than following the orientation of the existing building, the new volume runs perpendicular, with one extreme passing over the street.

Seibersdorf Offices and Research Center

Wolfgang Döring

1. Rolandsburg Hotel
   1988

2. Wabbel House
   1990

3. Stampfel House
   1995

3. Schickert-Schäfer House
   1997

Bielicky House 1994

Döring's architectonic solutions are explicit in content, though this does not make them obvious. He applies rigorous geometry to both the floor plan and the exterior volumetric study to resolve his proposals. There are no merely ornamental features in his facades to distort their interpretation; they simply stand there, white, bare, austere, and sometimes translucent. The details are taken from the formal repertoire of the modern movement, as in the case of the metal railings and sliding windows. Like in the work of Le Corbusier, concessions to color are addressed to specific instances in the building, like the red surface supporting the wash basins in Stampfel House. Other, less evident, situations are also revealed, such as the correspondence between indoor and outdoor spaces, which are designed as a single space, or the successions of planes in which the building's facades are organized. In other cases, the spectator is invited to walk through the architecture across narrow footbridges which burst into spaces and even into the facades.

Wolfgang Döring (1934) studied at the Technical University of Munich and at the Technical University of Karlsruhe, from where he graduated. In 1964, he was commissioned to restructure an old building in downtown Düsseldorf which was to be refurbished as a house for some art collectors, with the baroque facade—dating from 1683—being restored to its original state. Döring designed white spaces throughout as a neutral backdrop for the collection, his taste for the language of modern architecture being apparent. In his more recent projects, he has continued his contacts with the world of art, with six houses on the outskirts of Düsseldorf for gallery owners and other arts-related people. The houses follow a strict geometry in their design; their bare, white facades, in which the openings are completely controlled, continue to recall the works of the masters of the Modern Movement. Döring's professional praxis has also been applied to the fields of urban planning and interior design in several countries, including Germany, Saudi Arabia, Turkey, and Italy.

Bielicky House

- **Location:** Düsseldorf, Germany.
- **Construction:** 1995.
- **Architect:** Wolfgang Döring, Michael Dahmea, Elmar Joeresen.
- **Associates:** Georg Döring.
- **Photographs:** Manos Meisen.

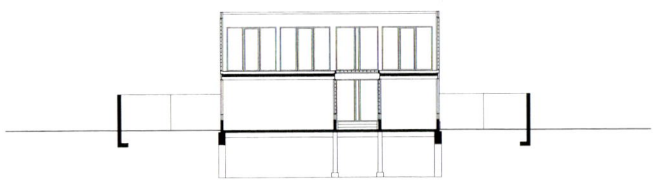

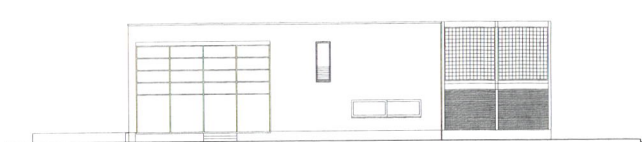

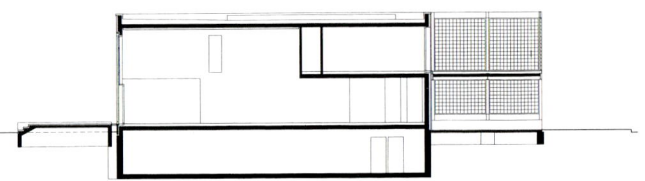

OBERGESCHOSS

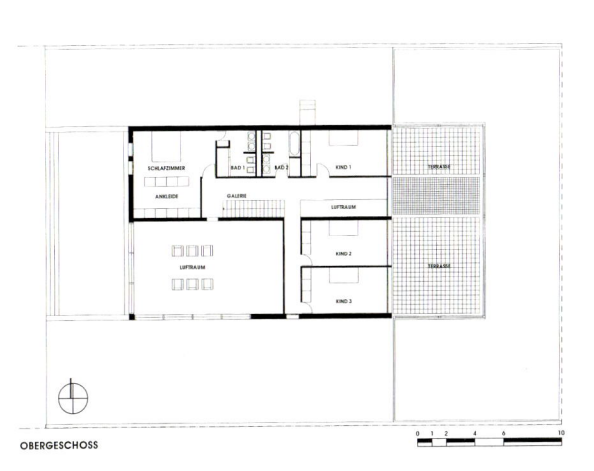

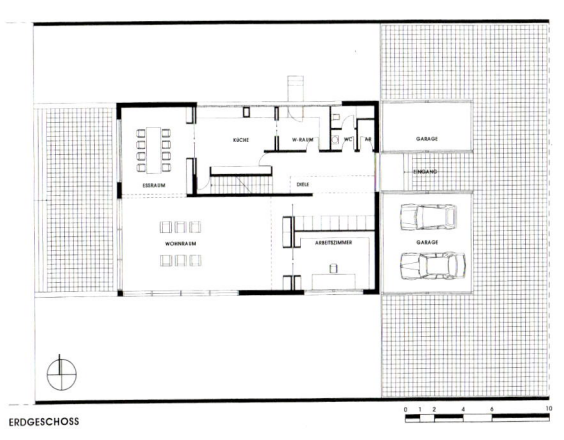

ERDGESCHOSS

Once again we are faced with an austere language which makes no concessions, with details inspired by the modern tradition (metal tube railings, narrow balconies, sliding windows, white walls). Once again the volume of the building is a perfect prism: no single element projects from the surface of the facade. What this house reveals most of all is Döring's interest in the skin of buildings.

Bielicky House | **35**

Carles Ferrater

1. House in Binisafua
   1990

2. L'Estartit Sailing Club
   1991

3. Housing in Vall d'Hebron
   1992

4. Housing in Barcelona's Olympic Village
   1992

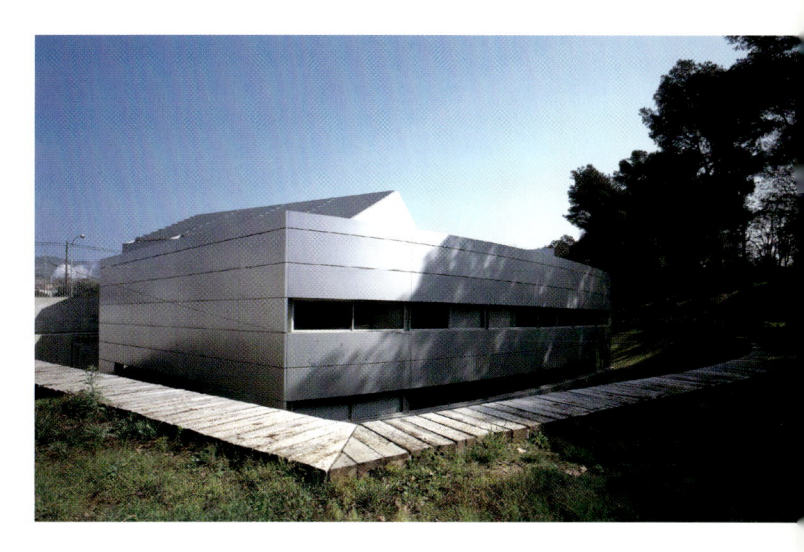

Baix Llobregat County Hall 1995

In a country like Catalonia, where there is a strong predominance of small offices over big architecture studios, Carles Ferrater is one of the architects with the largest volume of built work. While he has also designed public buildings, what stands out most is his capacity to develop private projects that manage to reconcile modern language with the more commercial side of architecture.

Carles Ferrater's skill lies in introducing markedly modern materials, typologies, and technical solutions into a mainly conservative market with a slight tendency to kitsch.

His built work is protean in nature: it is not just the size and budget of his projects that are variable (from a family house to a hotel with a fourteen-floor foyer); the form and the architectural concept behind them also differ widely, to produce projects with as little in common as L'Estartit Sailing Club and Sitges Market.

To some extent, this flexibility is due to the way the office works: Ferrater tends to involve teams of young architects in each of his projects; as a result, each proposal is produced by a different team of associates. Ferrater knows how to adapt to his client and the formal trends of a given moment.

Carles Ferrater (Barcelona, 1944) graduated from the Barcelona School of Architecture in 1971. Since then, he has lectured in Projects at the same university, and since 1973 he has based his professional practise in Barcelona. During the eighties, he designed several apartment buildings and family houses in L'Estartit: El Port building (1980), El Guix de la Meda House (1984), the Garbí building (1988), and Pasco de Molinet House (1988). For the Barcelona Olympic Games (1992), Ferrater planned two major housing complexes, used to accommodate journalists and judges during the event, and a large, privately-run hotel: the Juan Carlos I.

Shortly afterwards, he designed the hotel's gymnasium, an entirely subterranean building which establishes a very interesting relationship with the landscape and which, along with Castellón Technology Park (1995), is his major project to date.

He has been associated with Joan Guibernau since 1993.

Baix Llobregat County Hall

- **Location:** Torreblanca Park Precinct, Sant Just Desvern, Spain.
- **Construction:** 1994.
- **Developer:** Mancomunitat de Municipis de l'Área Metropolitana, Baix Llobregat County Hall.
- **Architects:** Carlos Ferrater and Xavier Güell.
- **Associates:** Joan Guibernau (associate architect), Luis Martín (project), Alfredo Santín (master builder), Gerardo Rodríguez (structure), Cooperativa del Baix Llobregat (construction company), Francisco Juncosa (installations).
- **Photographs:** David Cardelús.

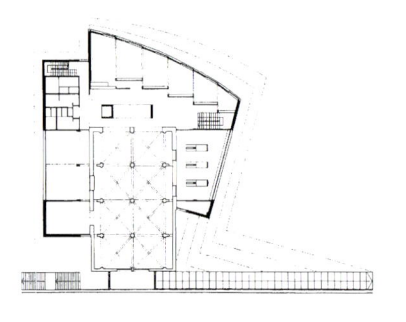

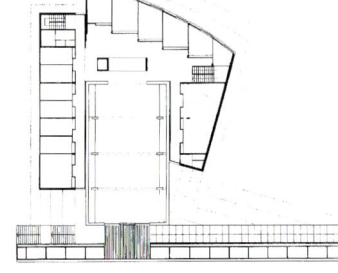

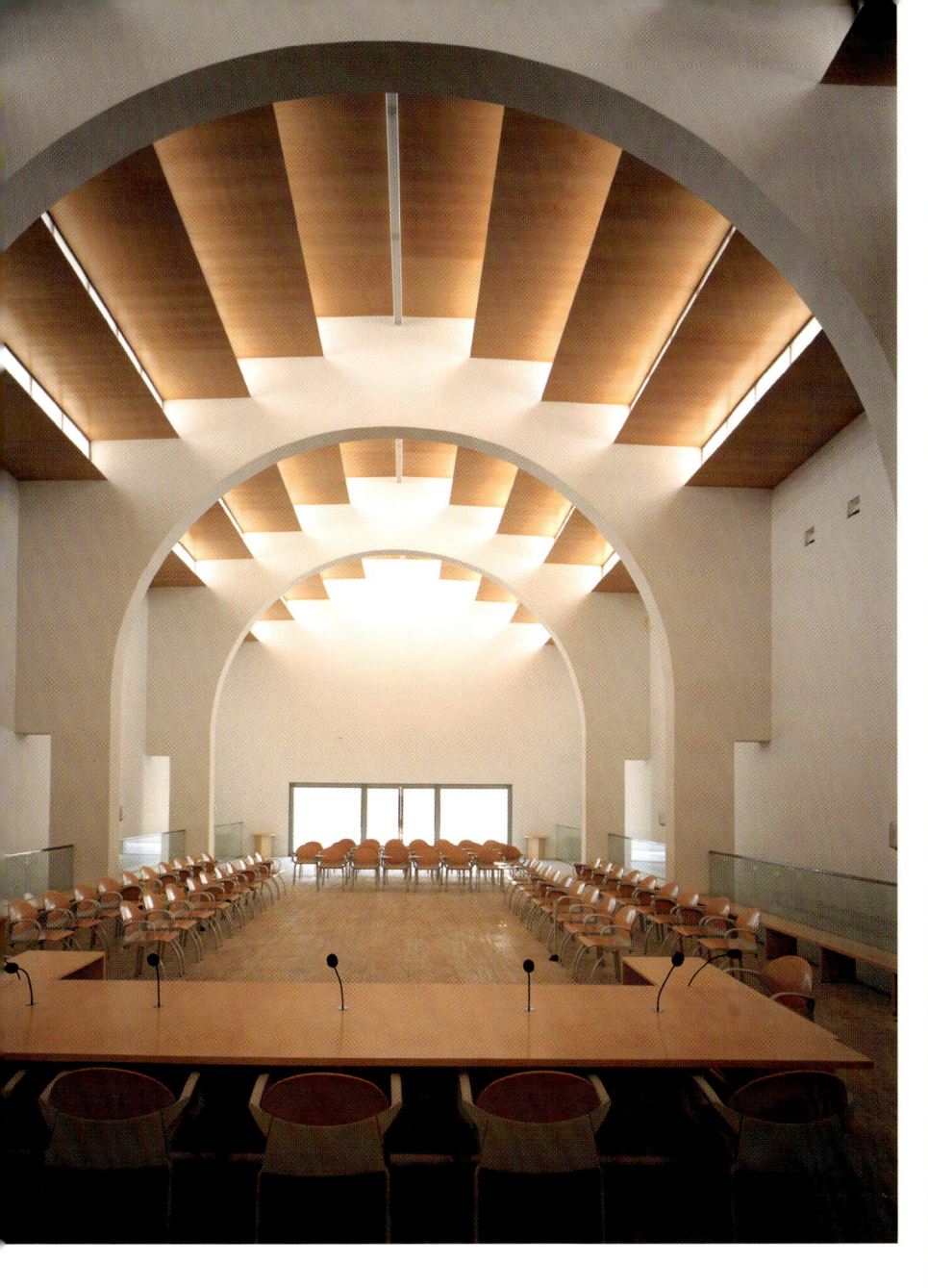

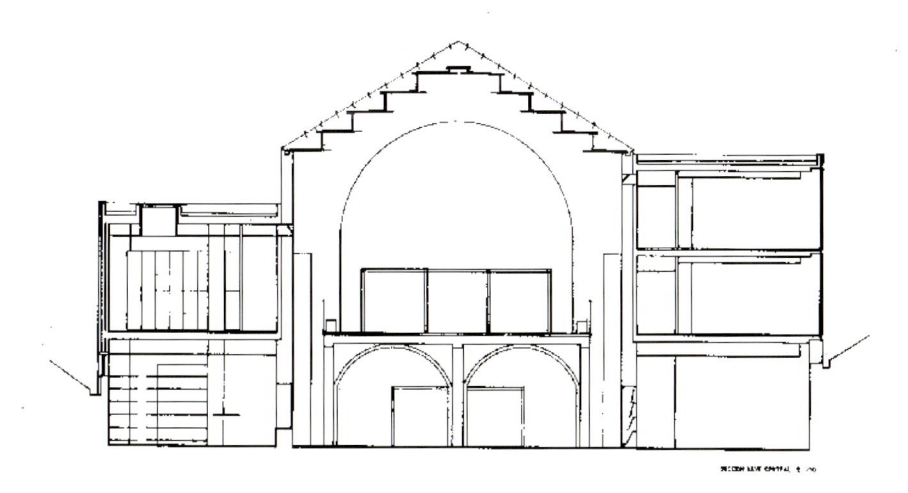

The channeling of daylight is one of the main themes in this project by Carles Ferrater. This page shows three different examples of methods used by the architect to draw light into the interior: a circular skylight, a breach running along the side facade, and a stepped roof which includes horizontal strips of windows.

Baix Llobregat County Hall **39**

Norman Foster

1. Hong Kong and Shanghai Bank
1986

2. Stansted Airport
1991

3. Bilbao Subway Station
1996

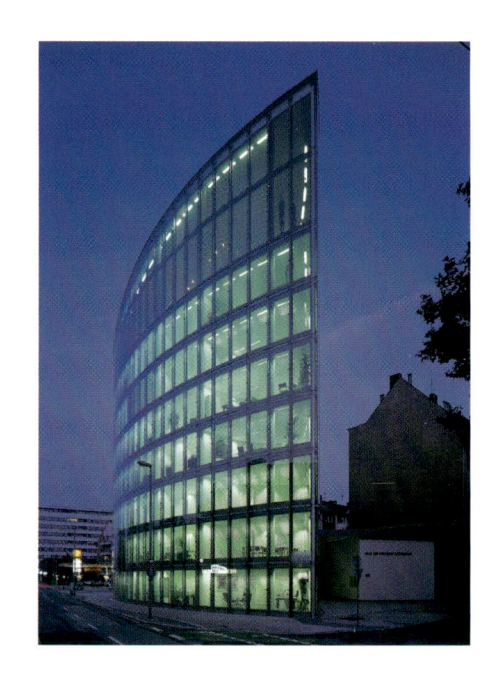

4. Development Center
1994

5. Commerzbank
1997

Law Faculty, Cambridge 1995

Between the semi-sunken family houses with roof gardens and great skylights which marked Norman Foster's early career and his recent major works, such as the Commerzbank building in Frankfurt or Hong Kong's new airport, there may be differences in scale, budget, management, and even image, but not in philosophy.

Norman Foster represents the optimistic side of technology. Ever since his early days with Buckminster Fuller, Norman Foster has always been interested in technology's capacity to improve the relationship between architecture and nature and to increase the comfort level of buildings.

In Foster's projects, technical display is never an end in itself; its purpose is to achieve greater control of lighting and environmental conditions. Although his work is often classified as high-tech, along with that of his most famous British colleagues, in Norman Foster we do not see an imitation of industrial imagery, as we do in Richard Rogers and Nicholas Grimshaw, or an attempt to fuse engineering and Victorian tradition, as in Michael Hopkins.

Norman Foster (Manchester, 1945) studied architecture in his home town before going on to Yale University. On his return to England, together with Richard Rogers and their respective wives, he formed Team 4, which was responsible for some innovative projects in the mid-sixties such as Brumwell House (1964) and the Reliance Controls Factory (1967), which immediately brought the team recognition.

The break-up of the group in 1967 coincided with his years of cooperation and friendship with Buckminster Fuller, his admittance to the Architectural Association, and the completion of various industrial projects. In the seventies, Foster started to concentrate on office design. The main office of Willis, Faber & Dumas (1974) was named best British building of the decade by the RIBA. His later work, with buildings such as the head office of the Hong Kong and Shanghai Bank, Stansted Airport, Tokyo's Century Tower, and Nîmes Mediatheque have all been well publicized and much spoken of. His present-day studio comprises some 300 professionals from different disciplines, with offices in London, Hong Kong, Glasgow, Berlin, Frankfurt, and Tokyo.

Law Faculty, Cambridge

- **Location:** University of Cambridge Campus, England.
- **Construction:** 1995.
- **Client:** University of Cambridge.
- **Architect:** Norman Foster.
- **Structures:** Anthony Hunt Associates.
- **Library capacity:** 120,000 volumes.
- **Photographs:** Herman H. van Doorn.

The new faculty—including five auditoriums, seminar and meeting rooms, offices, and an extensive library covering a total of 10,000 square yards—occupies six floors. Two of these are basement floors, ensuring that the faculty interferes as little as possible with the existing campus skyline. The ground floor houses multipurpose rooms, offices, and other staff areas. The basements are taken up by three large auditoriums, book deposits, and student meeting rooms, while the three top floors are set aside for the library proper.

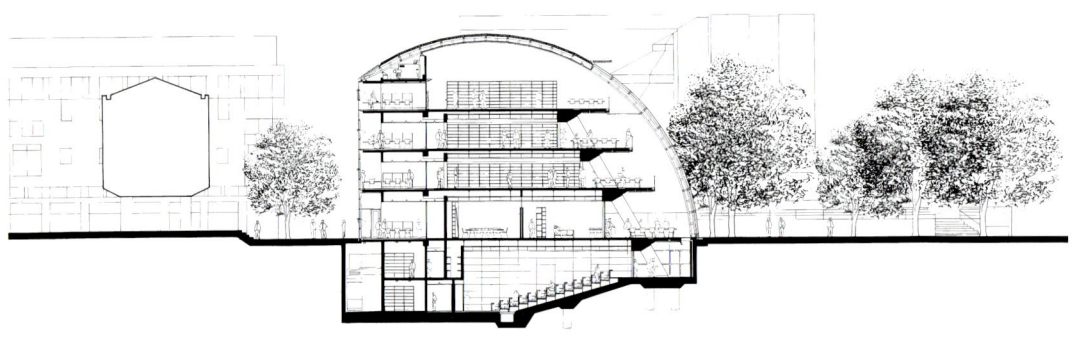

42 *Norman Foster*

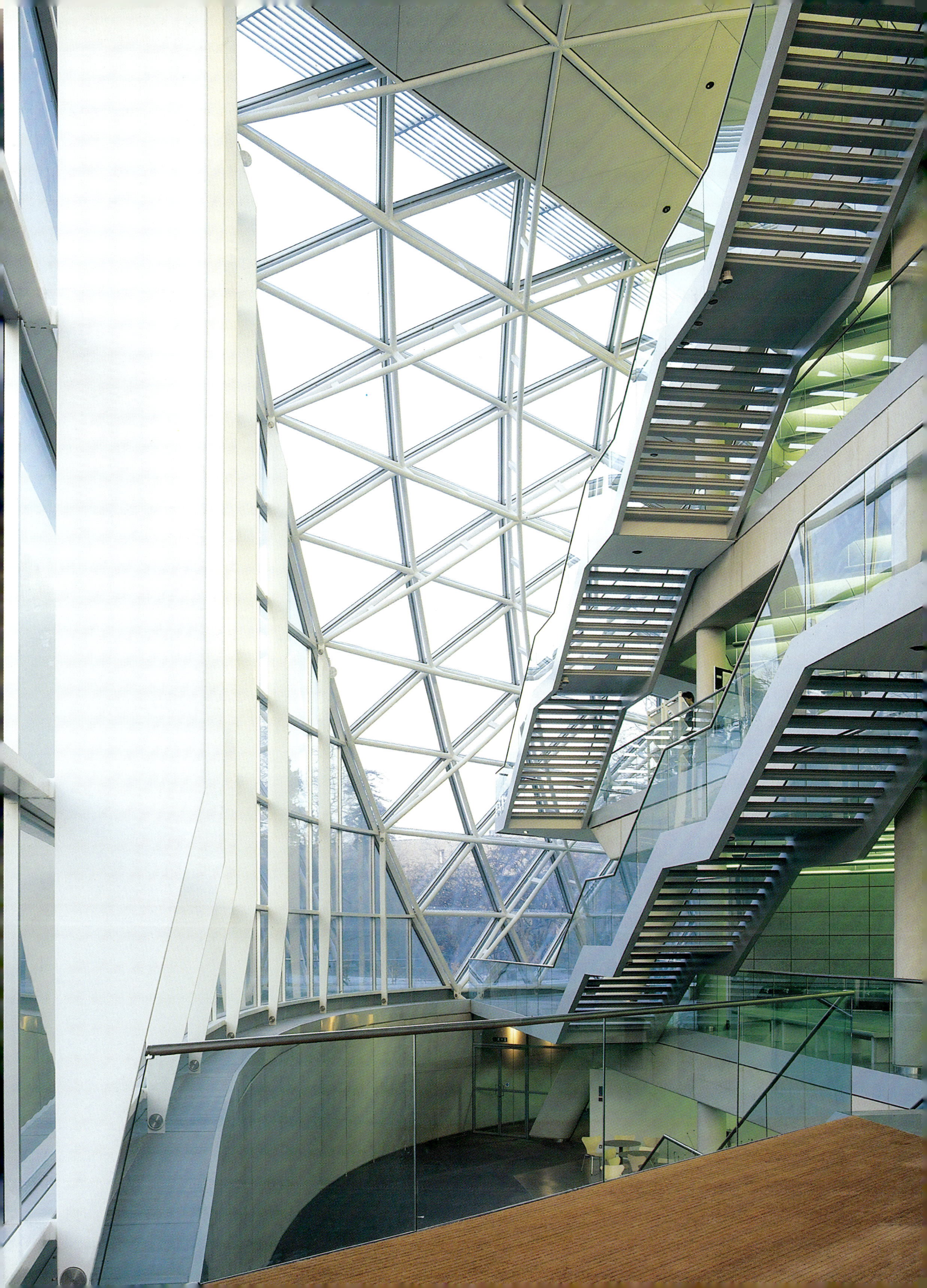

Frank O. Gehry

1. *Guest wing of Winton House*
   1987

2. *Vitra Museum*
   1989

3. *The Herman Miller Factory*
   1989

4. *Schnabel House*
   1989

44

Guggenheim Museum, Bilbao
1997

It is difficult to speak of a single Gehry, because there are really several: the Gehry who experiments with the perception of objects in perspective and the use in architecture of cheap and marginal materials such as wire fabric and cardboard; the Gehry who introduced figurative elements into architecture on the basis of Claes Oldenburg's ironic view of the consumer society and the change in scale of the most everyday objects; the Gehry who adopts the composition strategies of the Russian constructivists to articulate complex systems based on simple pieces; the Gehry who creates buildings of sinuous membranes thanks to the use of NASA information technology systems, etc.

There is a clear difference between the experimental exercises of his early projects, in keeping with the work of many of his artist friends, and the huge media coverage given to his present-day buildings. It almost seems as though Gehry has been trapped by his own capacity to surprise and construct disproportionate buildings. Clients come to his studio from all over the world to ask him for just that: spectacle.

Frank O. Gehry (Toronto, 1929) studied architecture in the fifties at the University of Southern California and at Harvard, while working with several professional studios. In 1962, he set up his own studio, Frank O. Gehry and Associates. During the seventies, he designed his series of cardboard chairs and armchairs. Also from this period are the hay barn in San Juan de Capistrano (1968), Ron Davis' Studio (1972) and the unbuilt series of Gunther, Familian, and Wagner Houses (1978) which, along with his own, completed in 1978, brought undervalued materials into the architectural limelight.

In the eighties, Gehry designed the space in Los Angeles for an exhibition about Russian constructivism. From then on, his architecture changed, and he started to work on the complex relationships between simple volumes. Forming part of this tendency are the Aerospace Museum in California (1984), Loyola Law School (1984), and the Winton and Schnabel residences.

In recent years, these simple volumes have undergone a gradual transformation. Their surfaces have warped, and their corners are less geometrical and more organic. This is the case of the Guggenheim Museum in Bilbao and the headquarters of Nationale Nederlanden in Prague.

Guggenheim Museum, Bilbao

- Location: Bilbao, the Basque country, Spain.
- Construction: 1997.
- Architect: Frank O. Gehry.
- Associates: Randy Jefferson, Vano Haritunians, Douglas Hanson, Edwin Chan.
- Photographs: Eugeni Pons.

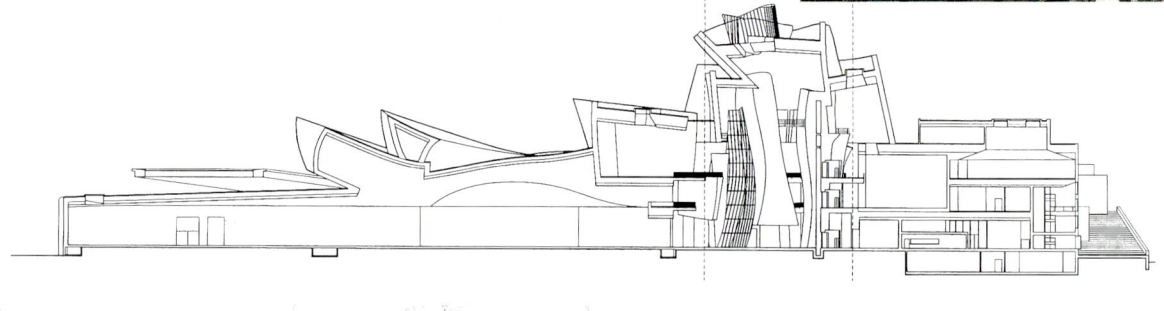

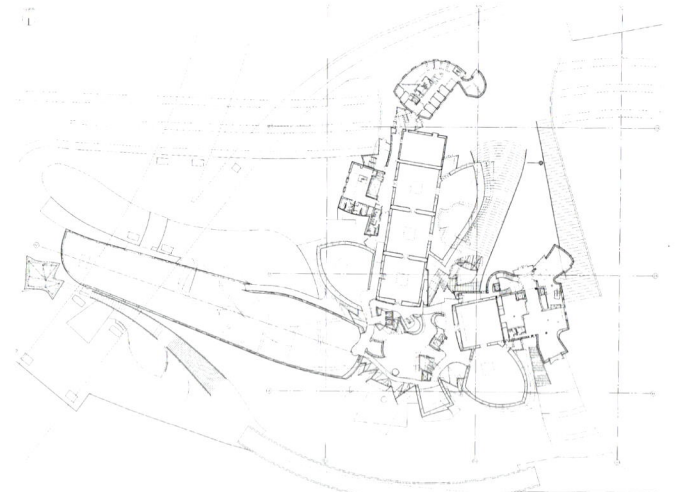

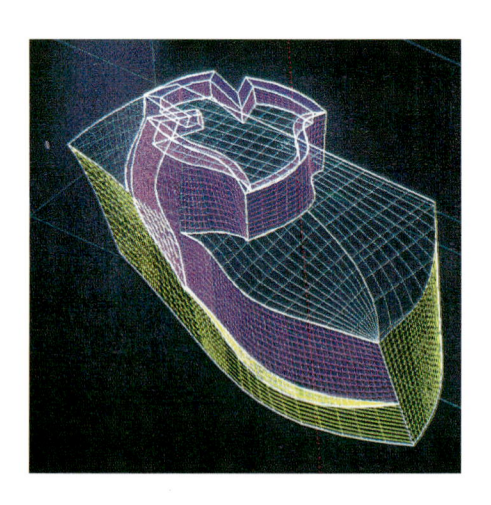

Gehry's project was selected after a limited competition which included the proposals of Arata Isozaki and Coop Himmelb(l)au. The Basque Government and the representatives of the Guggenheim Foundation were looking for a singular, iconoclastic building that would both repeat the impact made by the New York headquarters by Frank Lloyd Wright and become a focal point for the world of culture and project the city worldwide. In addition to its cultural function, the building was also intended to become a vast advertisement for the metamorphosis of Bilbao.

46 *Frank O. Gehry*

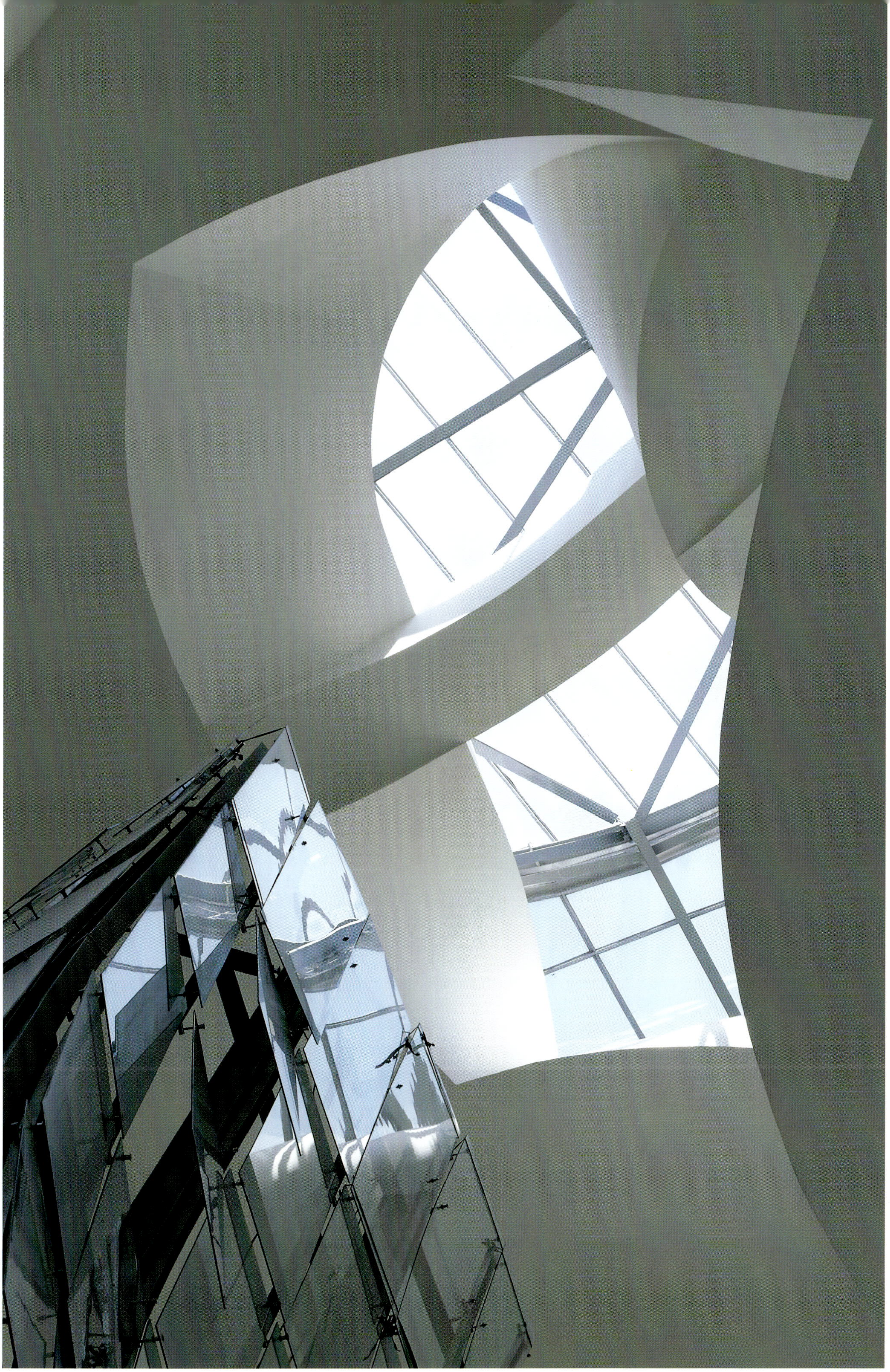

Peter Gluck

1. *Bridge House*
1996

2. *Linear House*
1996

House in Worcester 1995

This architect spent a period of his working life in Japan in the early seventies that has made a lasting impression on his work. His projects pay as much attention to detail as to composition; this is the result of the various conditioning factors to which the project is subject. This leads to a whole range of different possibilities: new and old are brought together in extensions to existing structures; the front-back concept of facades is seen as a basic element of design, as in Two-sided House; the limits between inside and out dissolve, as in Linear House; all of which leads to a definition of his architecture as contextual modernism. In any case, his buildings are profoundly rooted in their surroundings, whether natural or built. Each project adopts a certain solution, influenced by the client and the context; various formal codes are used, from the classical organization of the facades in Three-gable House (Lakeville, Connecticut, 1985-1989), or the rationalist rhythm of Manor House (New York, 1985-1989) to the cubic volume of Urban House (Brooklyn, New York, 1993).

Peter Gluck studied at the University of Yale. His professional practise started in New York, though he took some years off and moved to Tokyo where he worked for a construction consortium. From this moment on, his knowledge of Japanese culture was to influence his standpoint on the architectural question. Since 1972, Peter L. Gluck and Partners has been established in New York. His architecture is characterized by integration in the context and the relationships it strikes up with the various conditioning factors to which a project may be subject. Two-sided House in Lincoln (Massachusetts, 1980-1982) was an experiment into the different facades of one house, but it also reflects the value which Gluck attaches to the client's requirements. Two extensions to existing buildings have been landmarks in his career: in 1985, to Mies House in Weston (Connecticut) and in 1992, Wright's house for the United Services Organization in Pleasantville (New York). In 1993, he built Linear House, which explores relationships with local tradition.

House in Worcester

- Location: Worcester, New York, USA.
- Construction: 1995.
- Architect: Peter Gluck.
- Associates: Fritz Read, Jim Walker.
- Photographs: Paul Warchol.

In his design for the extension of a collection of various parts, Peter Gluck has managed to respect the scale of the house, despite doubling it in size. This is critical for the conservation of its bucolic image, which the owners were loath to give up. What is more, a different project, while preserving the old wooden house, might have converted it into a caricature of itself. The finishes and materials retain a distant echo of the old mansions from the last century: soft colors, brick walls, roofs of steel sheet varnished in a dark toasted tone, similar to the slate, picture windows shaded with jalousies. Without using images or objects from the last century, Peter Gluck has managed to capture the familiar domestic atmosphere of the neighboring house by taking geometry, a play of colors, and the combination of materials as his only means.

Michael Graves

1. Riverbend Musical Center
   1990

2. Private Home
   1992

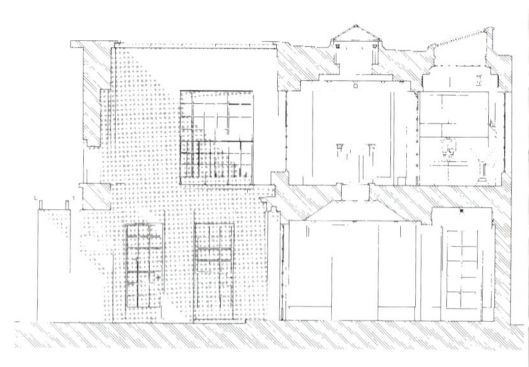

3. Denver Library
   1996

University of Cincinnati Research Center 1997

It was the work of Le Corbusier that inspired Graves' early projects, which take their place in the movements of purism and postcubism. After his project for Portland Town Hall (1980), however, color and facade came into their own, the former to overcome one of the prejudices of modern architecture, the latter as a pictorial and scenographic element. Here, the system of axes used in the ground plan and the free combination of elements inevitably recall the classical tradition. From then on, Graves was to become one of the main representatives of postmodern architecture.

The Portland building received a degree of criticism for its apparent indifference to setting, and this was to influence the course of Graves' later works. Today, context is one of the basic premises underlying his designs, to the extent that some of his recent projects can be likened to stories based around their setting and place, elements which he uses as the bare bones around which to organize the project.

Michael Graves (Indianapolis, 1934) studied architecture in the late fifties at the University of Cincinnati, Harvard, and the Rome Academy. Since starting out in practise in Princeton in 1964, Graves has developed from the neo-avantgarde abstraction of his origins to the postmodern language which characterizes his most recent works. His beginnings take us back to the time when he was known as one of the Five Architects, the other four being Peter Eisenman, Richard Meier, John Hejduk, and Charles Gwathmey. At the end of the sixties, the New York-based group endeavored to develop a similar theoretical basis to that of the European avant-garde movements of the twenties. Their aim was to free architecture from historical memory and the conditioning factors of functionalism, declaring its independence as an abstract practice.

In the late sixties, under the influence of Leon Krier's neo-classical speculation, and having produced various expansion projects which involved direct contact with history, his work started to feature classical and vernacular references alongside abstract forms. It is this combination of languages that defines his present-day architecture.

University of Cincinnati Research Center

- **Location:** Cincinnati, Ohio, USA.
- **Construction:** 1995.
- **Developer:** Cincinnati University.
- **Architect:** Michael Graves.
- **Associates:** KZF Inc. (associated architects), Smith, Hinchman & Grylls Assoc. (design), Hargreaves Associates (landscaping), Monarch Construction (construction company).
- **Photographs:** Timothy Hursley.

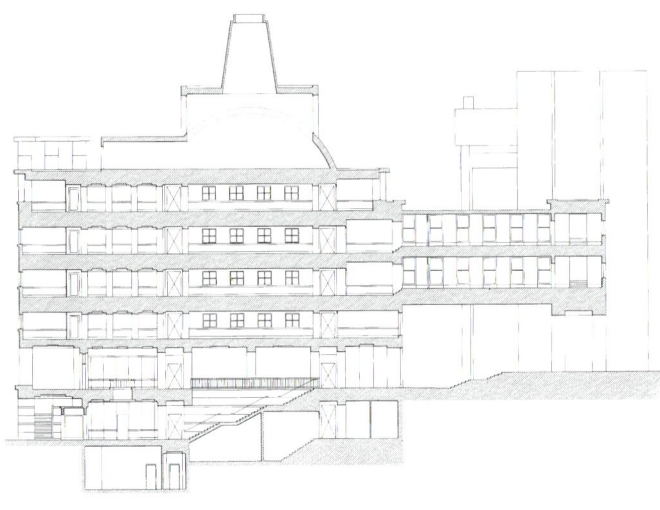

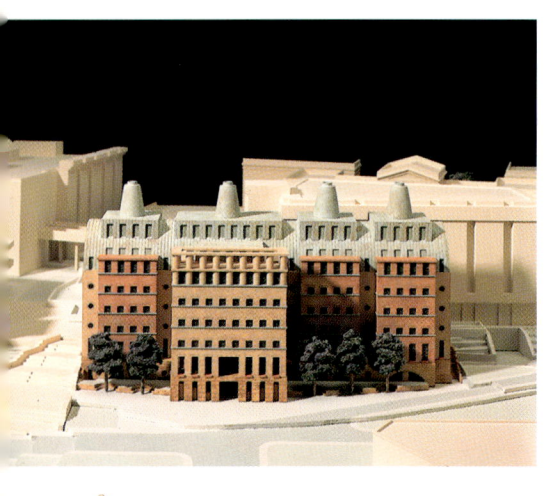

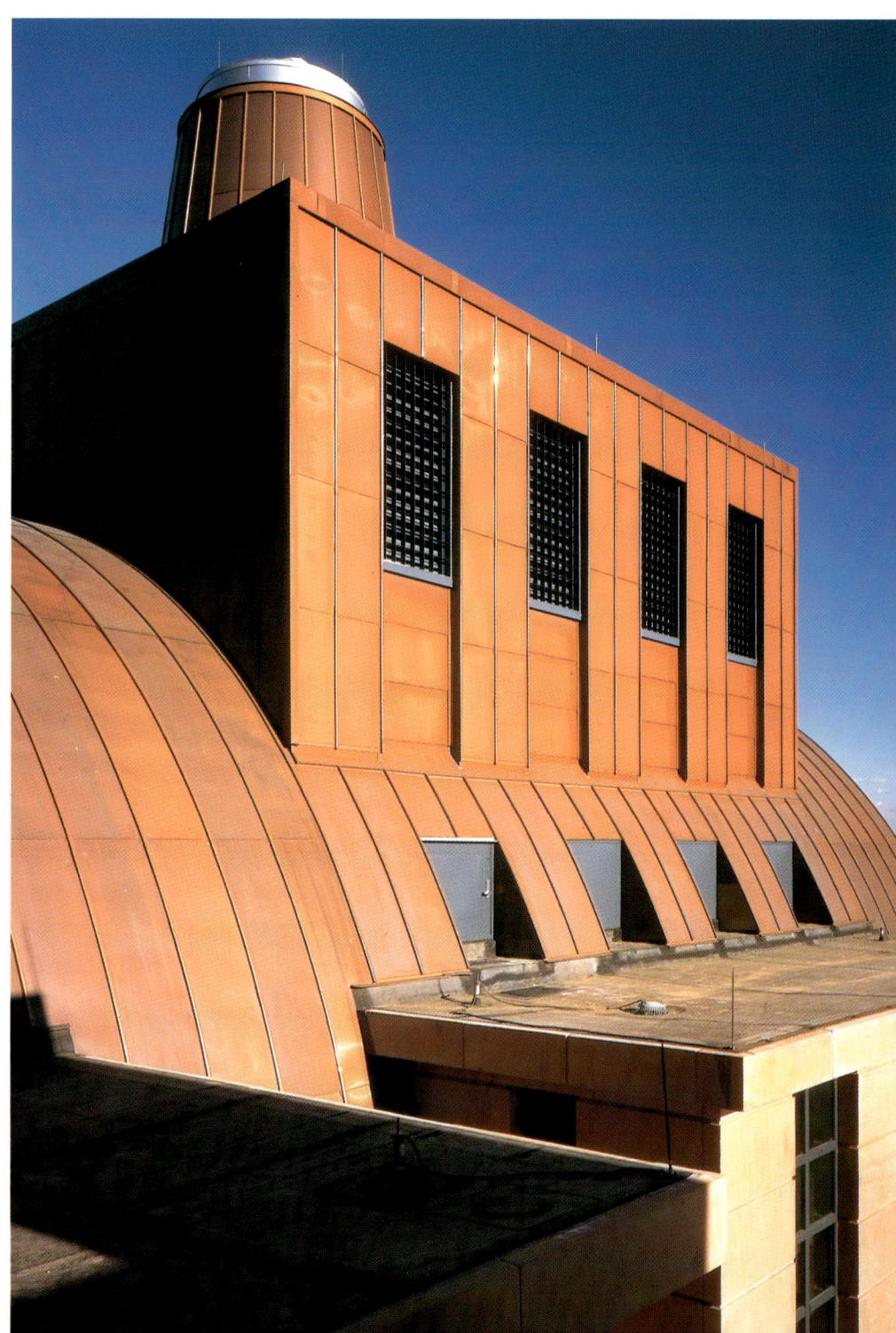

54   *Michael Graves*

In terms of volume, the building can be seen as the engagement of a great lengthwise pavilion and another four bodies arranged cross-wise, from which the entrance volume stands out. Despite the variety of materials used (ocher brick and terra cotta) and the shape of the windows (round and square), the facades convey a unitary order. The same discourse is repeated in the roof, clad with copper, in which industrial forms appear above a great lengthwise dome.

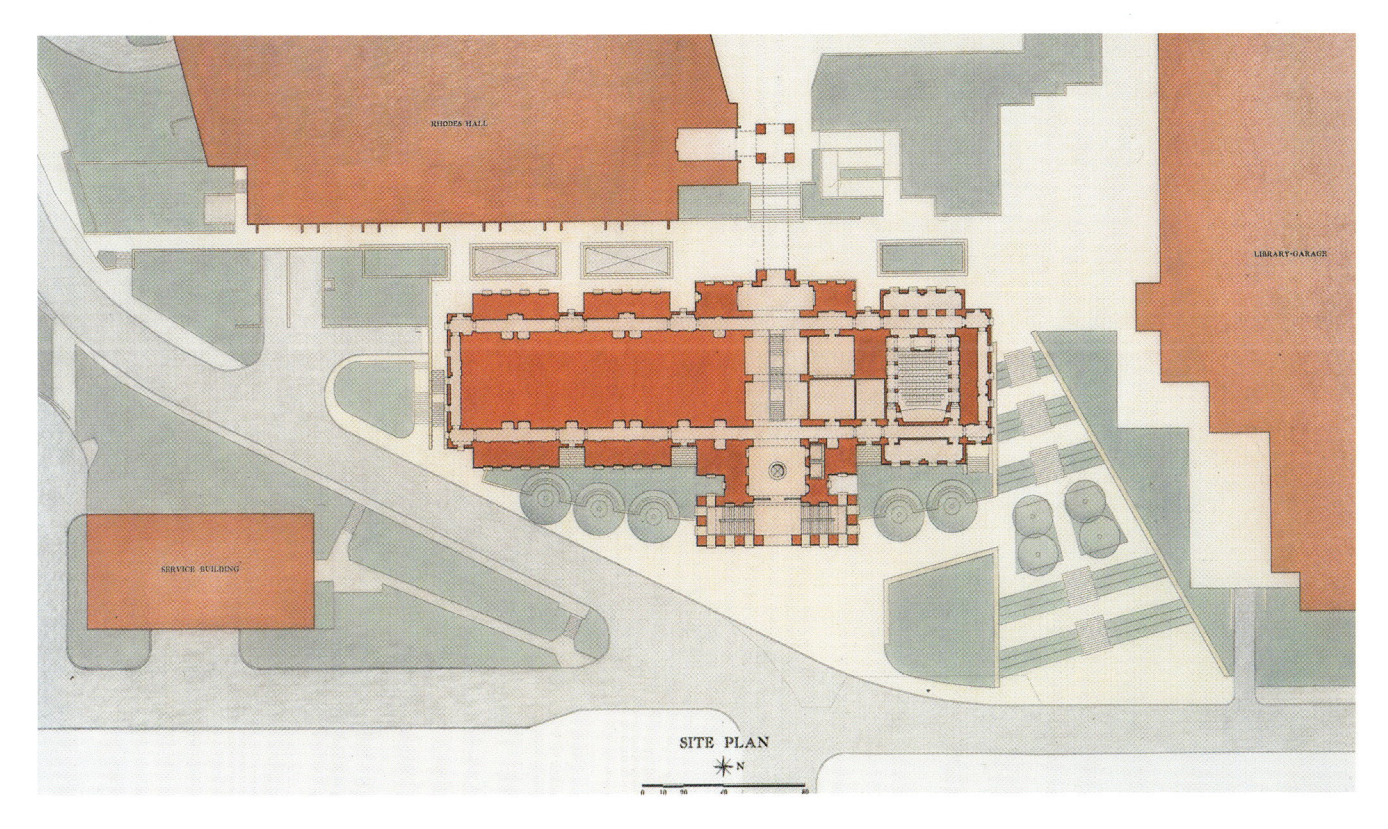

University of Cincinnati Research Center **55**

1. Heureka
1988

2. Finnish Embassy
1994

Home for the elderly in Vantaa 1993

Finland, where the figure of Alvar Aalto is still a vital reference on the architecture scene, provides the setting for the early career of these architects. Their projects focus meticulous attention on their surroundings and the landscape: this injects an interesting dynamism into their work, as their proposals are decomposed in terms of planimetry and form, only to be recomposed on a clear rationalist basis.

One of the constants in their career is their research into light, a question of paramount importance for Nordic countries and for Aalto himself. In the work of Heikkinen & Komonen we see their intention of introducing light throughout the building, at times using it to reveal what lies behind a glass facade, or even to build the "Analema de Sol" at Rovaniemi Airport. The project that brought them recognition was the Finnish Science Center (Heureka, 1986-1988), where the rigorous spatial order of the interiors becomes decomposition of volume on the outside. In their later projects, however, their taste for sober, elementary forms is much more manifest, to the point that they construct "container boxes" which, in some cases, develop their internal spatial movement in a single volume.

Mikko Heikkinen (1949) and Marku Komonen (1945) studied architecture at the Technical University of Helsinki, graduating in 1975 and 1974, respectively. In 1974 they set up Heikkinen & Komonen Architects. Throughout almost all of their career they have concentrated their work in Finland, where they have been responsible for major works, such as the Finnish Science Center (1986-1988) and Rovaniemi Airport (1988-1992). Since then, they have tackled smaller-scale projects, such as the Finnish Embassy in Washington D.C. (1990-1994), which have allowed them to construct more forceful buildings in terms of form. In recent years, they have moved definitively beyond the Finnish borders, taking part in the Prague Urban Planning project (1991), promoted by the Czech president, and the Matrix-H2O competition in Madrid (1992). Their studies on construction methods feature the Marimekko pavilion at the CPD Trade Fair in Düsseldorf (1993) and the construction of the Health Village in Guinea (1992-1994).

Home for the elderly in Vantaa

- Location: Vantaa, Finland.
- Construction: 1993.
- Developer: Foibe Foundation.
- Architect: Mikko Heikkinen & Marku Komonen.
- Photographs: Jussi Tiainen.

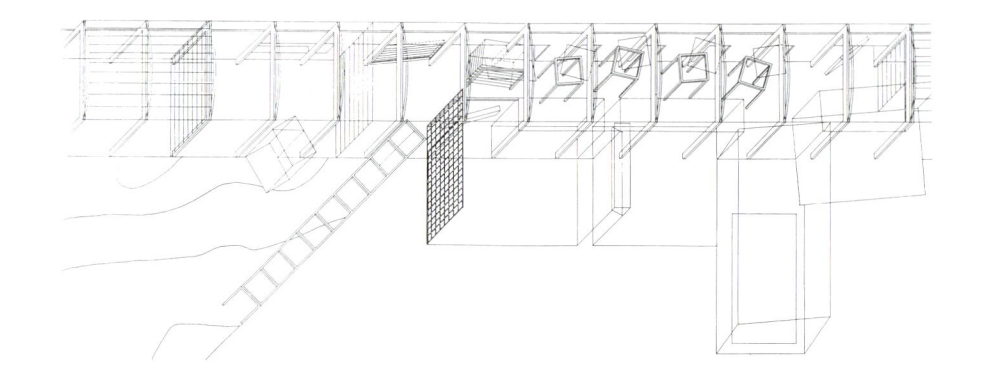

This home for the elderly is situated on the grounds of Rekola Villa, opposite Peijas-Rekola hospital. Although the buildings all belong to the same complex, the idea is to create some distance between the various annexes and set some buildings apart from others so that, rather than having the impression of living in a hospital, the senior citizens experience the spaces they inhabit as their own. The design of the residence is based on the same idea. The apartments have been divided into several blocks with all the communal services in an independent building. Each element or house has its own particular color, material, and volumetric study. They are not lined up in military fashion, but are distributed at whim, as Scandinavian villages are.

Home for the elderly in Vantaa

Herzog & De Meuron

1. Housing in Basel
1993

2. The Ricola Factory
1993

3. Railway Tower in Basel
1995

*Koechlin House
1996*

According to Herzog and de Meuron, our society tends to reduce the dimensions of space to its images—that is, to two dimensions. The development of a technical image has led to the loss of the magical one.

For Herzog and de Meuron it is vital to develop new strategies to contradict this distorted perception of reality and bring up new questions. In this sense, they are critical of the architects who act as advertising people, exploiting symbolic resources to update an architecture which does not necessarily have a conceptual or intellectual foundation.

For them, the main thing is to stretch and expand the limits of architecture, to extend its meanings, which are currently reduced to mere pragmatic techniques or, what is worse, postmodern graphic symbols. This means it is necessary to insist on the importance of the building as an object in itself and, therefore, to reclaim the specific qualities of architecture, such as the value of materials, the texture of the finish, and control of lighting.

Both Jacques Herzog (Basle, 1950) and Pierre de Meuron (Basle, 1950) studied at Zurich's ETH. After graduating in 1975, they stayed on as assistant lecturers to Dolf Schnebli until they founded their own architecture studio in 1977.

Since their first projects in the eighties, such as the photography studio in Weil-Fischingen, the stone house in Tavole, Vögtlin House in Therbill, and the Ricola Factory in Lustenau, the work of Herzog & de Meuron has stood out for its formal rigor and conceptual solidity. Their projects have had a marked influence on the growing interest expressed by many architects in the treatment of the skin of buildings and control of the texture of claddings.

In the nineties, Harry Gugger (Grezenbach, 1956) and Christine Bisnwanger (Kreuzlingen, 1964) joined the studio as new associates.

Koechlin House

- **Location:** Basle-Riehen, Switzerland.
- **Construction:** 1996.
- **Architect:** Jacques Herzog, Pierre de Meuron, Christine Bisnwanger.
- **Associates:** Jean Frédéric Luscher, Helmut Pauli (structure), Dieter Kienast (landscape), R+R Metalbau (windows).
- **Photographs:** Margherita Spiluttini.

Koechlin House is built from the inside out. The architects started working on the idea of a central court around which all the spaces in the house would turn. The perimeter of the court is completely changeable; depending on which screens are opened, it can occupy the entire ground floor or be limited to just the central nucleus. At the same time, the upper floor can be closed off with a sliding glass partition and used as a kind of conservatory when the temperatures start to fall.

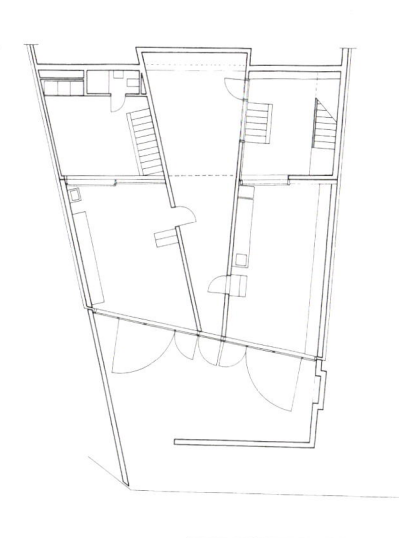

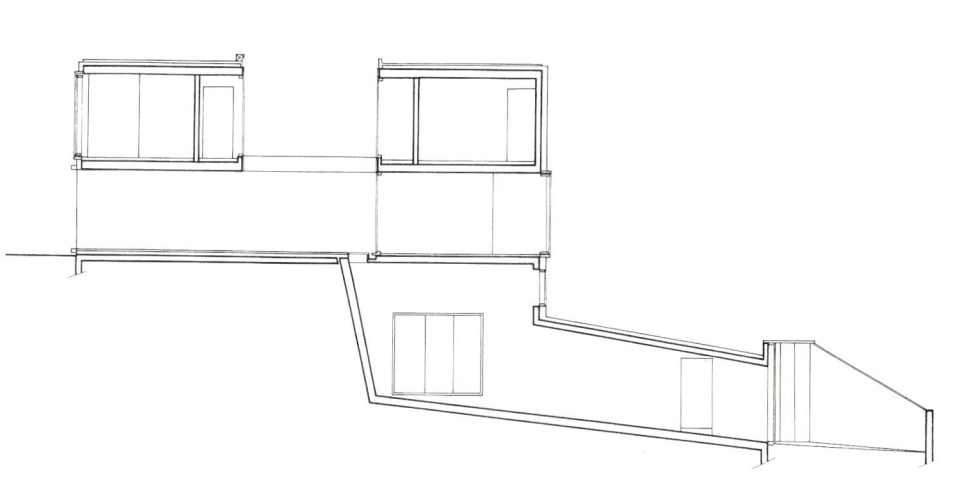

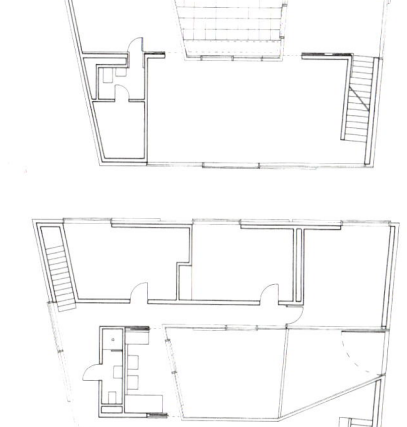

Koechlin House 63

Steven Holl

1. *Housing in Fukuoka*
   1991

2. *Housing in Makuhari*
   1996

St. Ignatius' Chapel 1997

Steven Holl has geared his personal investigation toward searching for closer connections between architectonic forms and their vital contents, to the point of proposing new concepts such as "articulated spaces", "silent openings", and "active structures". In the course of his research, Steven Holl has always sought a way to integrate the most diverse experiences in one project, to allow the coexistence of different moods in a single space. For this reason, he tends to complement his projects with diagrams which illustrate the main decisions, and with water-colors endowed with a high poetic content, in order to pick up the subjective meaning of architecture. In Steven Holl's work, nothing is immediate or obvious: the window frames, the mortar joints, or the openings effected in the walls create a calligraphy that is superposed on the building to emphasize the value of every corner and each detail.

Steven Holl (Bremerton, 1947) studied at the University of Washington and graduated in 1971. After a few years of professional practise in California, he set up his studio in New York and, shortly afterwards, joined the teaching staff of the University of Columbia. Although he often cites Scarpa and Wright as the direct inspiration for his work, the three architects are joined more by their attention to detail than by a literal similarity of form.

While Steven Holl's first projects and drawings, such as Berkowitz-Odgis House, are dominated by poetic imagery, particularly by the surrealist architecture of De Chirico, his work has gradually become more abstract and, to some extent, more architectonic. The poetry no longer lies in the images evoked, but in his treatment of spaces, his control of light, and treatment of the walls.

In this sense, his projects for the Storefront Gallery and an office foyer in New York summarize the main theme of Holl's later architecture: which form walls are to take. A question that, in his case, is not merely one of appearance, as it provides the basis for all of Holl's experiments with light and how to interrelate spaces.

St. Ignatius' Chapel

- **Location:** University of Seattle, Washington, USA.
- **Construction:** 1997.
- **Architect:** Steven Holl.
- **Associate architects:** Olson/Sundberg Architects.
- **Associates:** Tim Bade, Justin Korhammer, Jan Kinsbergen.
- **Photographs:** Paul Warchol.

St. Ignatius' Chapel, on campus at the University of Seattle, was built for the university's Jesuit community; therefore, the aim was to meet the requirements of the religious services of the Catholic Church. The constructed volume of the Chapel is set at the center of a virtual cross, all four arms of which comprise large green expanses with rectangular outlines so that the church seems to be the result of their point of intersection.

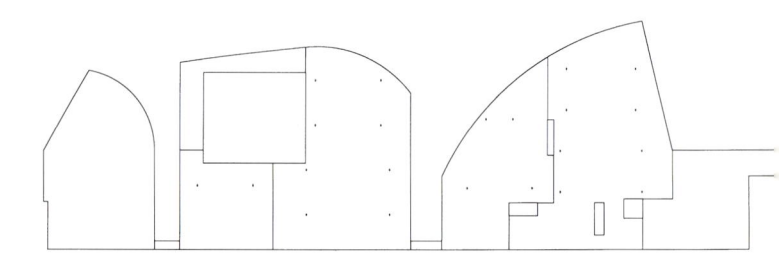

66 *Steven Holl*

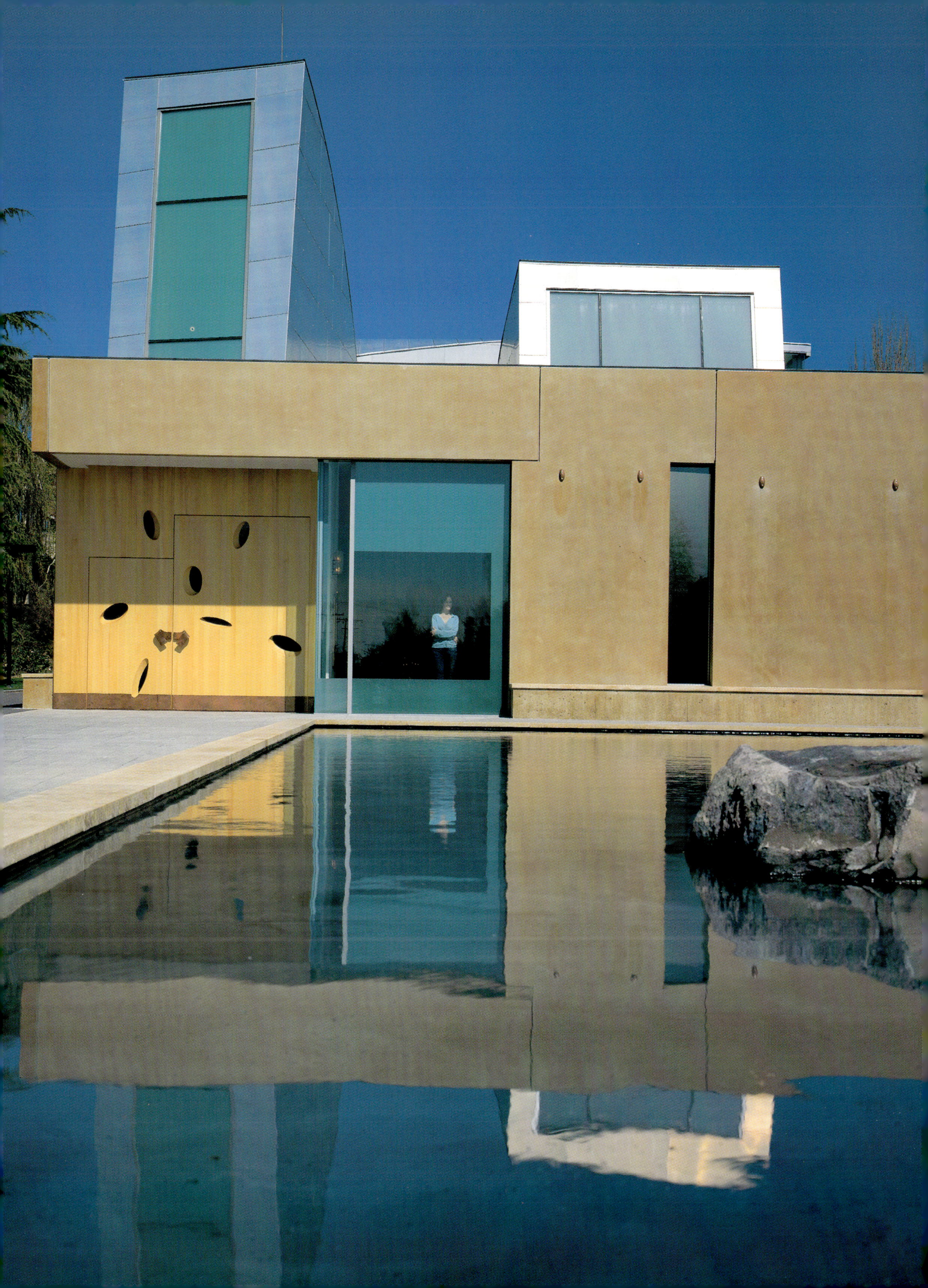

Arata Isozaki

1. Tsukuba Square
1983

2. Sant Jordi Stadium
1992

3. Domus. The House of Mankind
1995

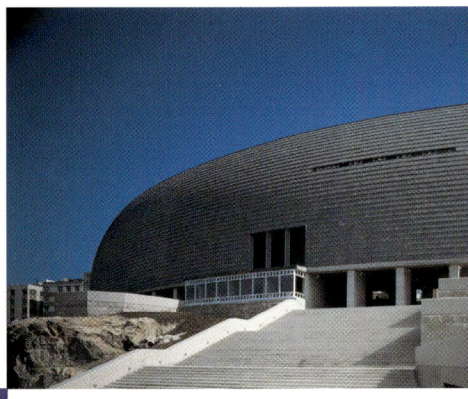

5. Japanese Center in Cracow
1994

4. Palafolls Sports Pavilion
1996

68

*Kyoto Concert Hall
1995*

In spite of the mutual attraction that Western and Japanese architects profess each other, the two societies' cultural differences set them so far apart that attempts at integration rarely go further than purely superficial questions of image.

In recent decades, Arata Isozaki has become the best represented Japanese architect in the Western world, thanks surely to his ability to fuse the two traditions more effectively than any other architect.

His admiration for Western urban design and classical tradition, with its axes and orders, has led him to a flirtation with post-modernism. Yet, in Isozaki's architecture, classicism runs deeper than image and becomes a way of promoting the system of analytical, rational thought so characteristic of European culture.

At the same time, Isozaki picks up the restraint and spiritual vocation of traditional Japanese architecture. This enables him, perhaps, to combine projects such as the Disney offices in Florida with tremendously lyrical works like the Ukichiro Nakaya Snow and Ice Museum (1995) and Domus in La Coruña (1995).

Arata Isozaki (Oita, 1931) studied architecture in Tokyo and began his professional practise under the guidance of Kenzo Tange. Regarded as one of the foremost Japanese architects of the generation following his teacher's, his work is an indisputable reference for younger architects. In the seventies, he formed part of the Metabolist movement, advocating the creation of major urban infrastructures that would allow ever changing buildings to adapt around them. Prominent projects from this period are those for Oita Central Library (1964-1966), the middle school in the same city (1964) and, above all, the plan produced in conjunction with Tange and Kurokawa for Tokyo City Planning (1960).

This movement had a direct relation with the structural thought of Levy-Strauss and the architecture of Archigram, Candilis, Bakema, and Hertzberger, and also reflected a brutalist sensibility along the same lines as Jean Dubuffet's theories.

His later works are no longer governed by such strict theories. Isozaki has become an intellectual architect who bases his projects on a conscientious study of the cultural context. This makes his work an architectural interpretation of his particular way of seeing each setting.

Kyoto Concert Hall

- **Location:** Kyoto, Japan.
- **Construction:** 1995.
- **Client:** Kyoto City Hall.
- **Architect:** Arata Isozaki.
- **Associates:** Hiroshi Aoki, Fumio Matsumoto, Hiroki Kitagawa, Rokuro Muramatsu, Naoki Inagawa, Jun Aiba, Igor Peraza (competition). **Contractor:** Joint Venture of Shimizu Corporation, Tokyu Construction, Kaname Co., Okano.
- **Photographs:** Katsuaki Furudate, Yoshio Takase.

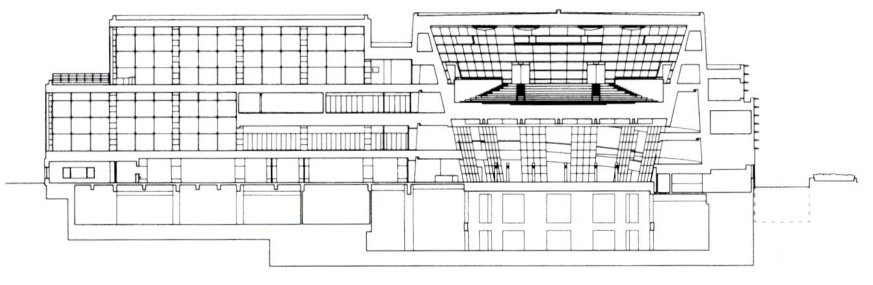

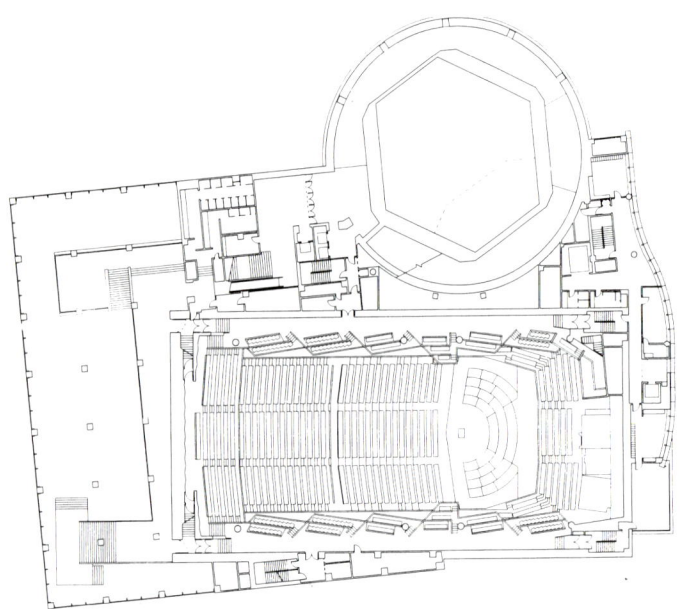

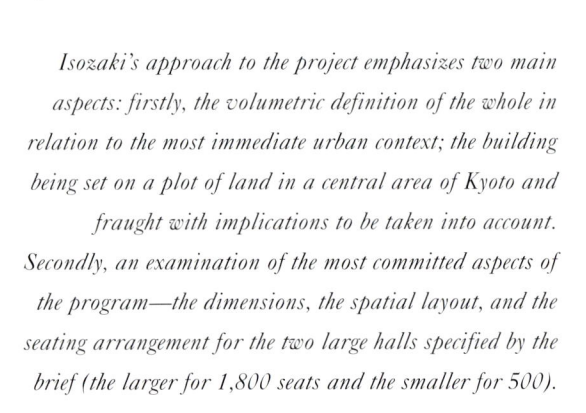

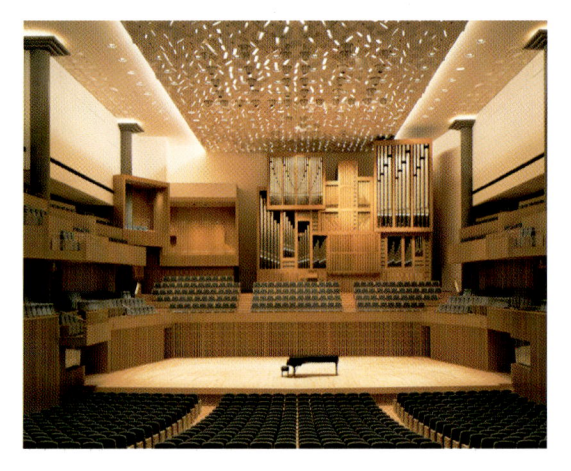

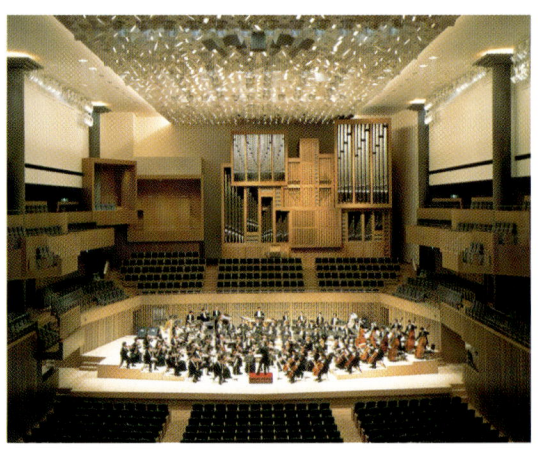

Isozaki's approach to the project emphasizes two main aspects: firstly, the volumetric definition of the whole in relation to the most immediate urban context; the building being set on a plot of land in a central area of Kyoto and fraught with implications to be taken into account. Secondly, an examination of the most committed aspects of the program—the dimensions, the spatial layout, and the seating arrangement for the two large halls specified by the brief (the larger for 1,800 seats and the smaller for 500).

70 *Arata Isozaki*

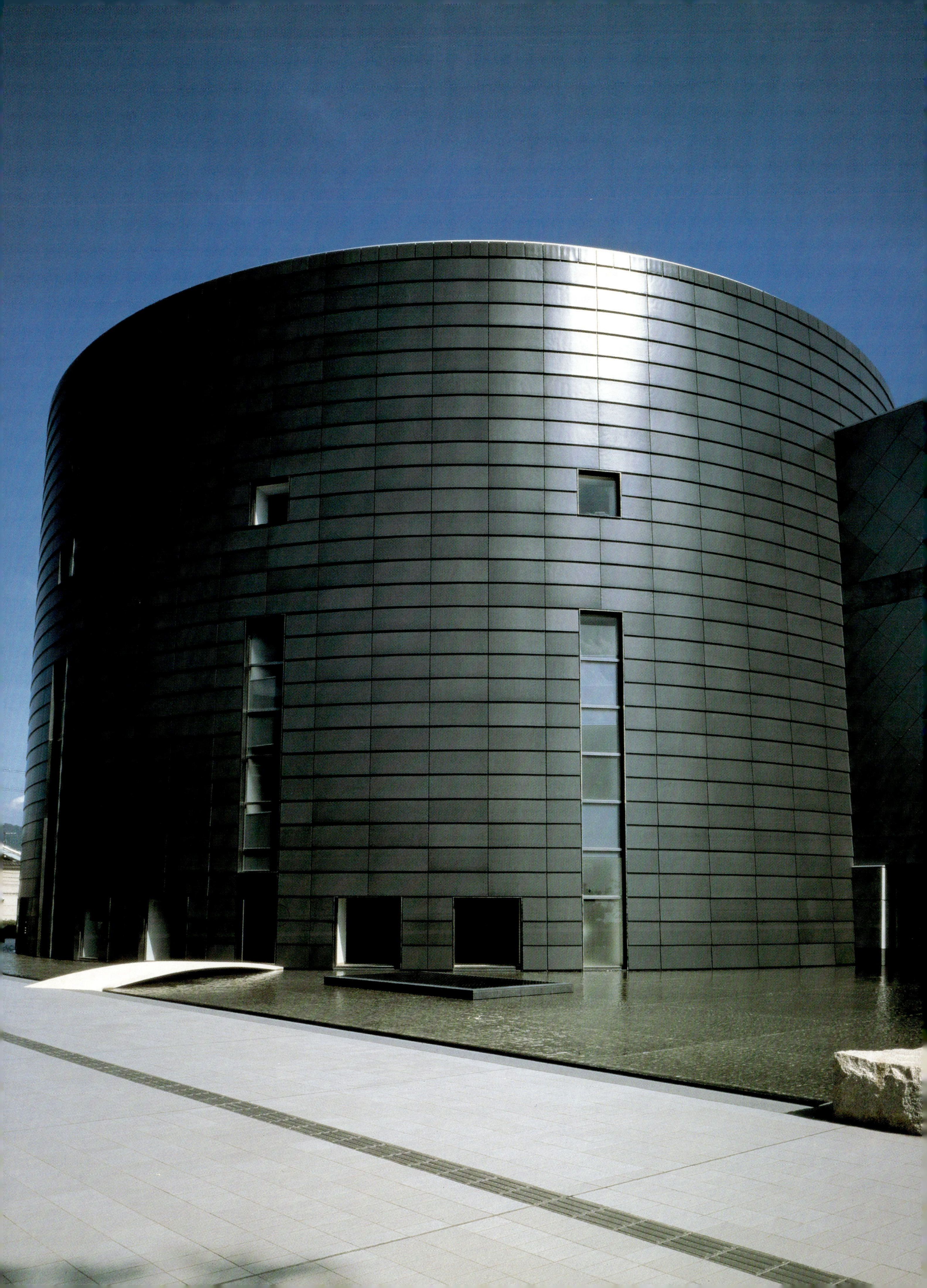

Toyo Ito

1. Tower of the Winds
   1986

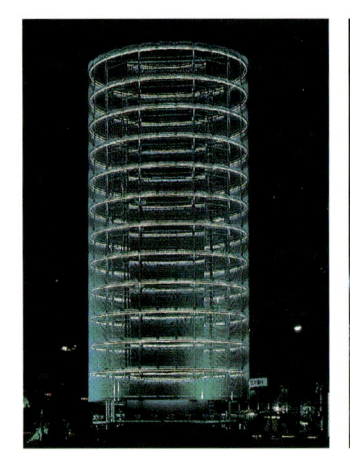

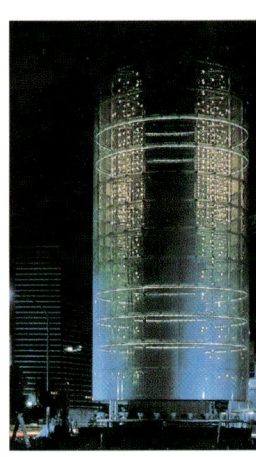

2. Sapporo Guest Wing
   1991

3. S House
   1997

*Nagaoka Auditorium
1997*

Ito's projects explore and develop light, transparency-filled architecture. Ito has always been particularly attracted by the ephemeral. Projects like his proposals for Experimental House for a Nomad in Tokyo, the series of mobile restaurants, and The Tower of the Winds in Yokohama all point to his affinity with the evanescent and the variable. In a way, Ito expresses the gap between architecture's rhythm and consumer-society's haste to renew and render obsolete what was just in fashion.

Even in his most costly projects, like the mediatheque in Sendai, he employs strategies such as transparency and the superposition of different planes to boycott any possibility of an unequivocal, static image. His allusions to mediatic, virtual reality are particularly frequent. Information technology and the development of communications have led people to see the world with different eyes, and it is the role of architecture, according to Toyo Ito, to interpret this new spirit.

Toyo Ito (1941) is one of the best known and internationally renowned Japanese architects of today. Yet despite being the same age as Ando, fame and major commissions have come later to him. In 1971, Ito set up his studio Urban Robot (URBOT), which was renamed Toyo Ito & Associates in 1979. His projects have always had an experimental edge to them. While in his early projects, White U House (1976) or the house in Kasama (1981), Ito worked with the limits of space and the positioning of sources of light, in the mid-eighties, he started to develop an architecture based on differing degrees of transparency, which crystallized in his designs for Silver Hut (1984), the Tower of the Winds (1986), and his nomadic projects.

Ito's architecture changed scale in the nineties. Commissions for the city museums of Yatsuhiro (1991) and Shimosuwa (1993), the fire station in Yatsuhiro (1996), and the Nagaoka Auditorium not only represented a great step forward in his career but also involved an inevitable change of strategy, channeled via the use of information technology and mediatic resources in building design.

Nagaoka Auditorium

- Location: Nagaoka, Nigata, Japan.
- Construction: 1994-1997.
- Architect: Toyo Ito.
- Program: Concert Hall (capacity for 700), Theater (capacity for 450), Studios.
- Structures: KSP-Hanawa Structural Engineers Co. Ltd.
- Photographs: Tomio Ohaschi.

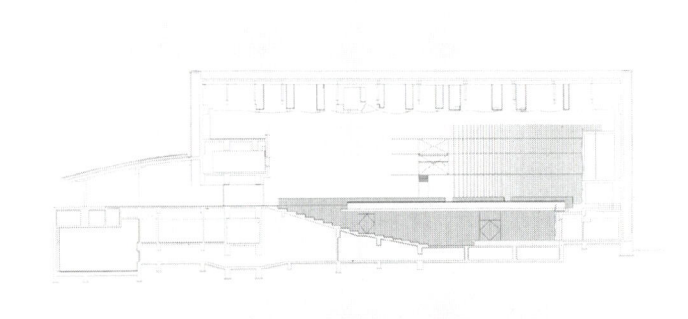

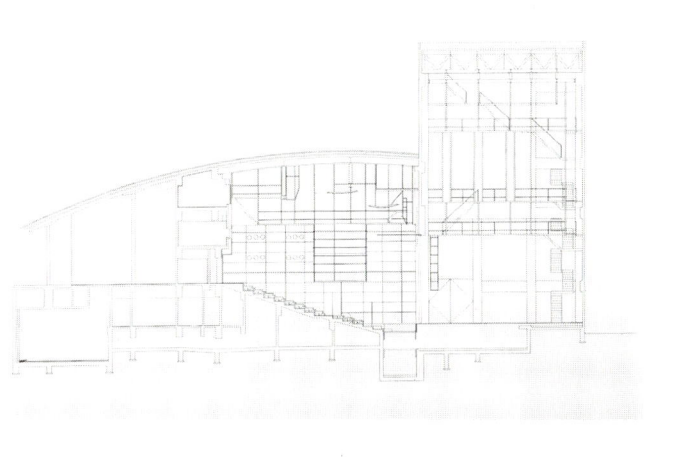

Nagaoka Auditorium 75

Helmut Jahn

1. One Liberty Place
1987

2. O'Hare Airport
1987

3. Hitachi Tower
1993

Kempinski Hotel
1996

A year after arriving in the United States (1966), this German architect started working for the firm C.F. Murphy Associates in Chicago, whose designs clearly pay tribute to the architecture of Mies van der Rohe. But Jahn's architectonic proposals gradually left Miesian aesthetics behind, as a result of his explorations in the technological field during his studies at the Illinois Institute of Technology. His projects began to deal with other architectonic principles, which were to mark the firm's new style after 1982, when Jahn became the main partner.

In his revision of history, he has reinterpreted the classic canons, to piece them back together in a new logic which comes close to the aesthetics of postmodernism and which, along with the great machinery of technology, characterizes the image of his projects, ranging from airports to Chicago high-rises.

Helmut Jahn (1940) studied architecture at the Technical University of Munich. In 1966, he left for the United States where he studied at the Illinois Institute of Technology under the eye of prominent theoreticians of technology. In 1967, he became an associate of the firm C.F. Murphy Associates in Chicago, where he eventually became president. Almost all of his work has been designed for Chicago, the home of his first skyscraper, the Xerox Center (1977-1989), and it is infused with a high degree of geometric abstraction. He also planned the One South Wacker (1979-1982) and the great high-tech container, State of Illinois Center (1979-1985). His work has since extended to other parts of the United States, with examples in New York, Texas, California, etc. Outside the States, he designed the Messe Frankfurt Convention Center, Hyatt Hotel (Frankfurt), and 362 West Street in Durban (South Africa), all clearly marked by his personal style.

■ Kempinski Hotel

- ■ Location: Munich, Germany.
- ■ Construction: 1996.
- ■ Architect: Helmut Jahn.
- ■ Associates: Peter Walker (landscape).
- ■ Surface area: 412,000 sq. ft.

Kempinski Hotel is the first building in the neutral zone of Munich Airport, given over to commercial and business activities and designed as a city within the airport. It is modular in nature, and forms part of a series of constructions which are still at the planning stage. The hotel is laid out in keeping with the airport's system of levels. The bedrooms, a total of 400, surround a central covered garden.

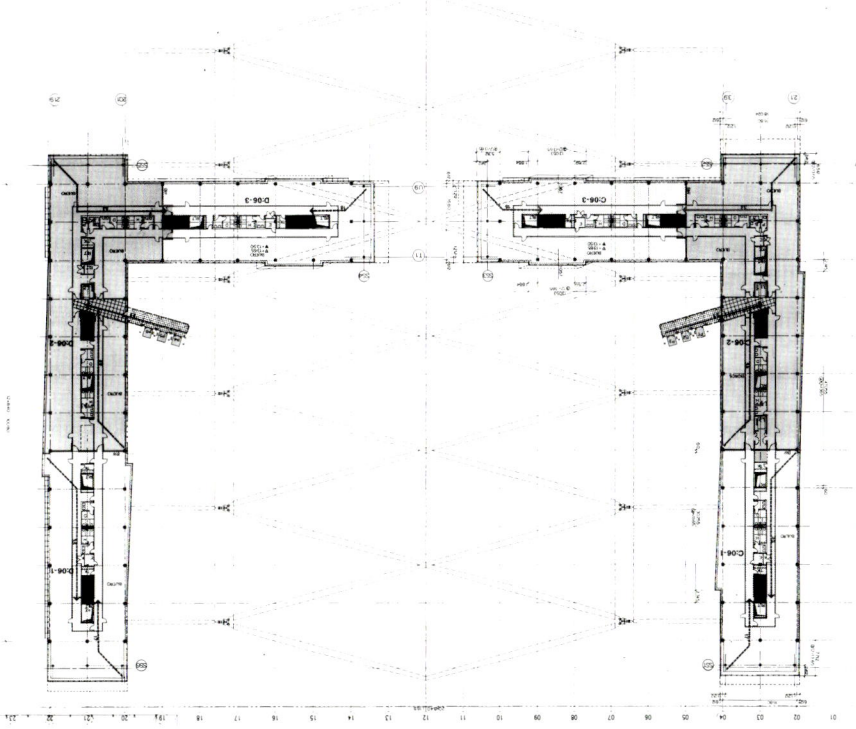

Kempinski Hotel 79

Jourda & Perraudin

1. Lyons School of Architecture
1987

2. House in Valse
1988

3. Venissieux-Parilly Station
1993

Housing in Lyons 1993

In the early works of Jourda & Perraudin we see reminiscences of art nouveau and Guimard's construction tradition, a general tendency toward the construction process and the use of materials. In some cases, the structure acts as a filter that allows us to glimpse the building's anatomy; in others, it is shown off as an envelope. Their versatile use of materials sees them applied to both construction and the creation of the architectonic image. In the social housing they designed for Tassin, the concrete used on the lower levels serves as a base for a great roof; the concrete buttresses extended to give greater privacy to the first-floor gardens. Beneath these great roofs are volumes of pure geometry, freely ordered to create an image of great lightness.

Françoise-Hélène Jourda (1955) and Gilles Perraudin (1949) studied at the Lyons School, graduating in 1979 and 1970, respectively. Later, they would build there the School of Architecture (1982-1987), in which we can see their interest in means of construction and materials. Some of their houses present the image of volumes beneath great roofs, as is the case with the single-family house in Lyons-Valse (1987). Their studies of form have delved into nature, particularly for the urban furniture, so reminiscent of great metal skeletons, such as the sign-posting in the Lyons subway (1989-1991), which resemble the Paris subway stations designed by Guimard. Their grounding in engineering has also allowed them to design bridges (Pont de L'homme de la Roche, 1989-1990). One of their most prominent works is the Parilly Subway Station (1982-1992) in Lyons, which stands out for its use of iron and concrete. Subsequently, they took part in the competition for Gerlaud Subway Station (Lyons, 1991), where a great volume emerging from the ground becomes the subway mouth.

Housing in Lyons

- **Location:** Lyon, France.
- **Construction:** 1995.
- **Client:** OPAC, Lyons.
- **Architect:** Hélène Jourda and Gilles Perraudin.
- **Associates:** Gavin Arnold, EZCA, Claude Brenier, Catherine Vardanégo.
- **Photographs:** Georges Fessy.

The system of stairways and corridors is comprised of a singular concrete meshwork added onto the rear facade, offering a completely superposed image. At both ends, this element includes the stairways leading to the various floors, but its expressive show is much greater than mere functionality requires, as the corridor surface is increased to produce a very important space for the building; it runs between the outer concrete screen and the plane of the facade. This space, where the inhabitants go up and down, walk to the elevators, or enter or leave their homes is presented as a collective area of community relations for the entire block, with its own life and specific qualities.

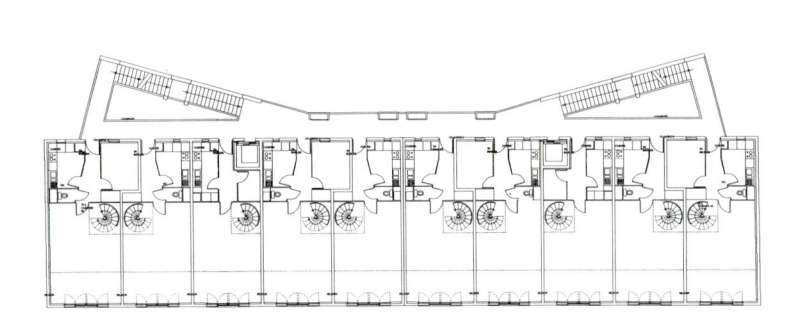

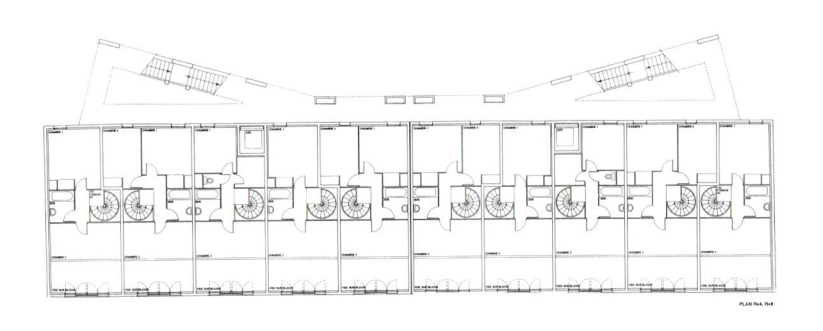

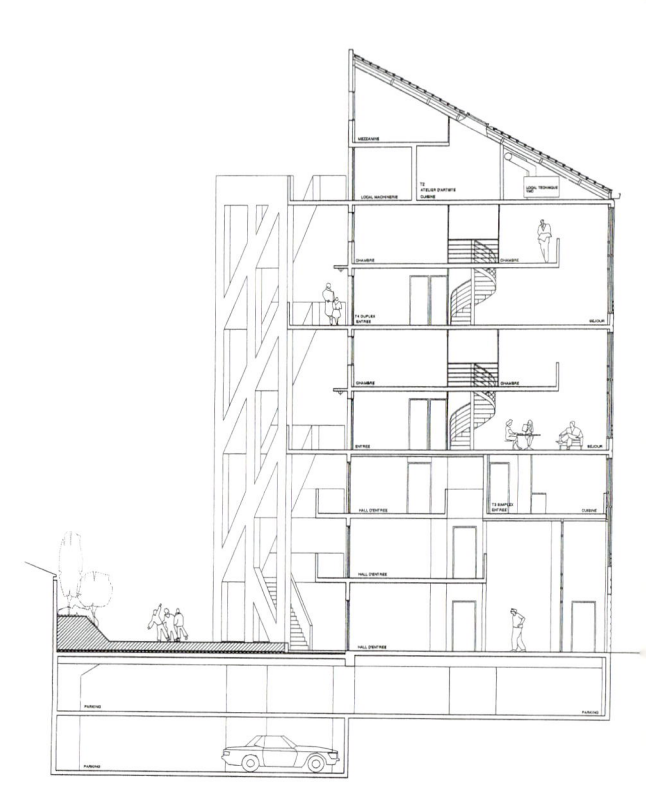

Jourda & Perraudin

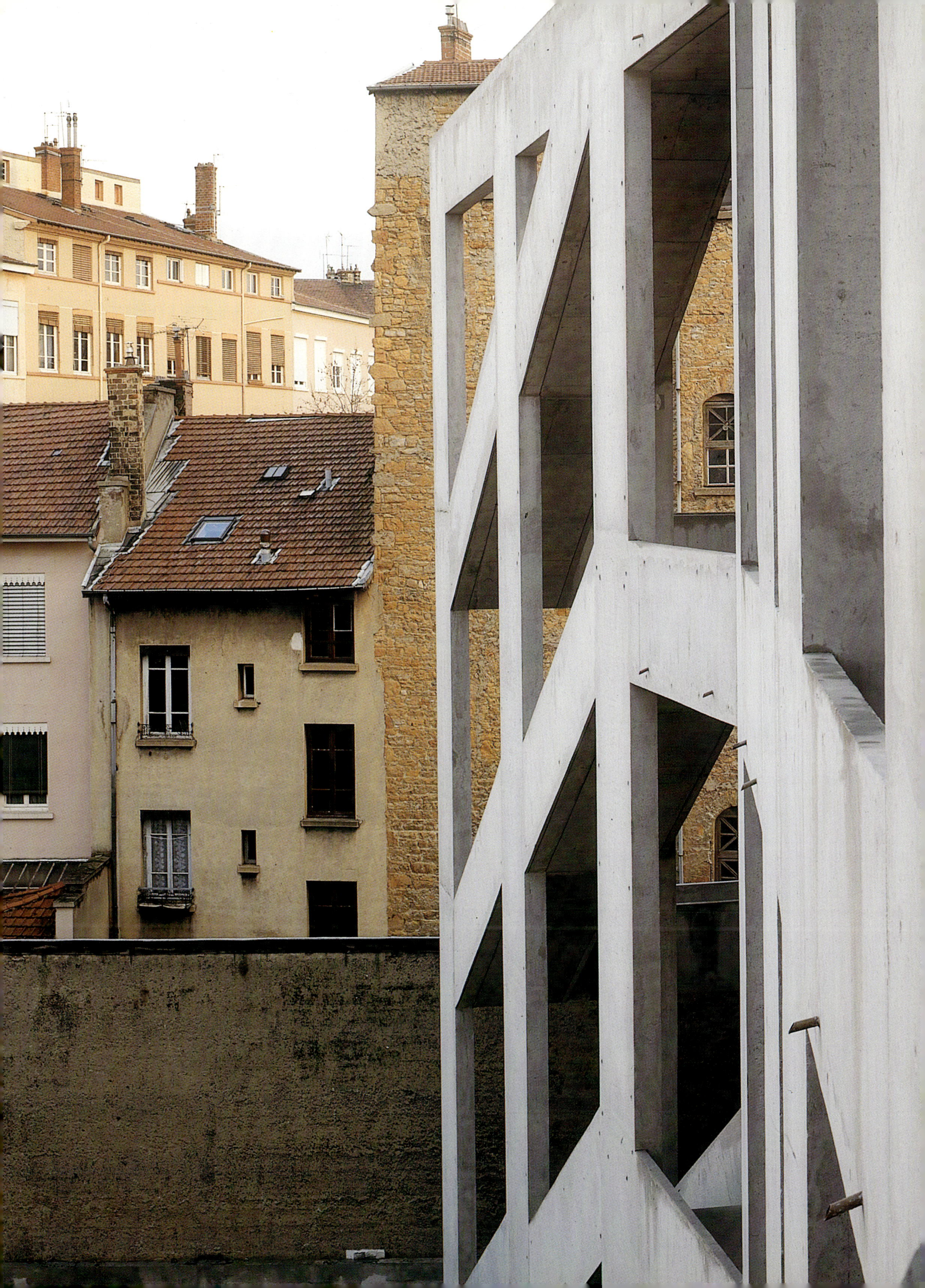

Rem Koolhaas

1. Patio Villas
1988

2. Dance Theater
1987

3. Grand Palais, Lille
1994

*Kunsthal Museum
1992*

Koolhaas' work takes a new look at modernity in a country with a major modern tradition. When postmodernism was carrying all before it, Koolhaas' criticism of the modern movement took a completely different form, based on the inherent complexity of the contemporary city, the simultaneous overlapping of systems at several levels, and the coexistence of contradictory readings.

However, his architecture suspends belief in the truth of the modern language rather than directly denying it. Koolhaas provides a hedonistic, libertarian interpretation of the architecture of the first half of the century, picking up its proposals without aiming to subscribe to its rational criteria and will to order. He is aware that historical events have undertaken to mercilessly destroy the utopia of a better society.

The primary objective in Koolhaas' work, from his writings to his projects and buildings, is to discover the connection between architecture and freedom which determines each decision in every scale, from the domestic to the urban, from the diagram to the detail.

Rem Koolhaas (Rotterdam, 1944) studied architecture at the AA in London—where he went on to become a lecturer—and at the IAUS in New York, during Peter Eisenman's time there. Koolhaas has always been connected with the theory of architecture, as lecturer at the innovative AA, as a speaker, and with his published work: Delirious New York, a retrospective Manifesto for Manhattan (1978) and the recent S, M, L, XL (1995).

In 1972 Koolhaas set up the OMA (Office for Metropolitan Architecture), whose name clearly expresses the planning intentions of the team, comprising Koolhaas, Elia and Zoe Zenghelis, and Madelon Vriessendorp.

At the OMA, the unbuilt projects are just as important as the constructed works, as all of their proposals involve implicit theoretical and critical considerations which are valuable in themselves. In fact, his built work is not very extensive in relation to his international fame and his influence on many young Dutch and Belgian architects: Willem-Jan Neutelings, MVRDV, Mecanoo, West 8, Xaveer de Geyter, Stéphane Beel, etc.

■ **Kunsthal Museum**

■ Location: Rotterdam, Holland.

■ Construction: 1992.

■ Architect: Rem Koolhaas.

■ Associates: Fuminori Hoshiho, Tony Adams, Isaac Batenburg, Leo van Immerzeel, Herman Jacobs, Jeroen Thomas and Patricia Blaisse. (interiors and garden).

■ Photographs: Lock Images.

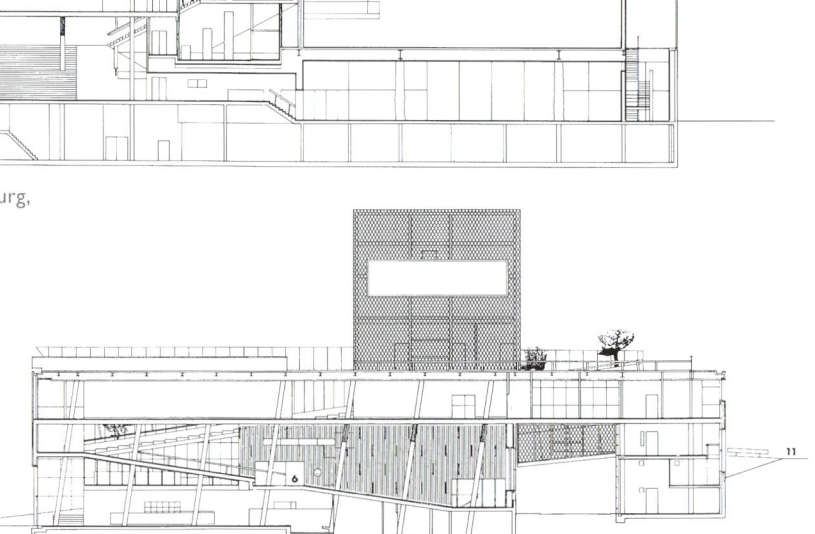

Rem Koolhaas

This museum is a coherent synthesis of several well-known modern precedents, the most obvious being Mies van der Rohe's National Gallery in Berlin. Here, the visitor leaves the street behind by going up a stairway to an immense concrete plinth where all the cultural amenities are laid out. This rise to a second plane of reference is based on the sequences leading into Renaissance churches, where the stairway raises the parishioner from the profane to the sacred. Having entered the building and walked around its galleries, visitors find themselves back outside on a kind of plinth, though a very different one to Mies': it projects from the building at street level, seeming to connect with it. This final stretch creates a sensation of ambiguity and surprise, apparently putting visitors out into the midst of the traffic.

Kengo Kuma

1. Observatory in Kirosan
   1994

2. Yusuhara Visitors' Center
   1994

The House of Water and Glass 1995

Along with Shigeru Ban and Kazuyo Sejima, Kengo Kuma is one of the most interesting Japanese architects of the generation following Tadao Ando and Toyo Ito. His latest works display an unusual capacity for working with architecture's least tangible elements: light, water, air, and landscape. His projects are light and seek transparency.

In an essay entitled "To See and be Seen", Kengo Kuma maintains that architecture has to establish a new relationship between subject and object, a relationship that goes beyond the idea of the building as a representative object. This calls not only for modern materials and the development of innovative forms, but also for experimentation with new ways of seeing. In this sense, his most representative project is the House of Water and Glass in Shizuoka: a system of transparent, translucent skins which creates a completely new relationship between spaces. The shadows, duplicities, and reflections produced are used to define itineraries and frame nature without actually establishing a clear-cut division between inside and out.

Kengo Kuma (Kanagawa, 1954) studied architecture at the University of Tokyo and graduated in 1979. In 1987, he set up his own architecture studio, first under the name Spatial Design Studio and, since 1990, Kengo Kuma & Associates.

Kuma's early works were set within the postmodern movement. His M2 building in Tokyo is particularly worthy of mention, an enormous, ironic pastiche of arches and columns, crowned by a gigantic Ionic capital. However, shortly afterwards his work left behind these stylistic idiosyncrasies to concentrate on less formal and more subtle aspects such as transparency.

His works from the mid-nineties onwards -Yusuhara Visitors' Center (1994), Kirosan observatory in Ehime (1994), the Japanese pavilion at the Venice Biennial (1995), Tomioka Lakewood Golf Club in Gunma (1996), and most of all the House of Water and Glass (1995)- saw a radical turn-about in his career.

Since 1985, Kengo Kuma has combined his work as an architect with lecturing at universities such as Hosei and Columbia.

The house of Water and Glass

- Location: Shizuoka, Japan.
- Construction: 1995.
- Architect: Kengo Kuma.
- Photographs: M. Fujitsuka.

The House of Water and Glass, which is mainly intended to house guests, contains a built surface area of 12,000 sq. ft. over three floors, occupying half of a plot of land of 13,800 sq. ft. It is situated on a cliff-top over-looking the Pacific Ocean, on the Atami coast.

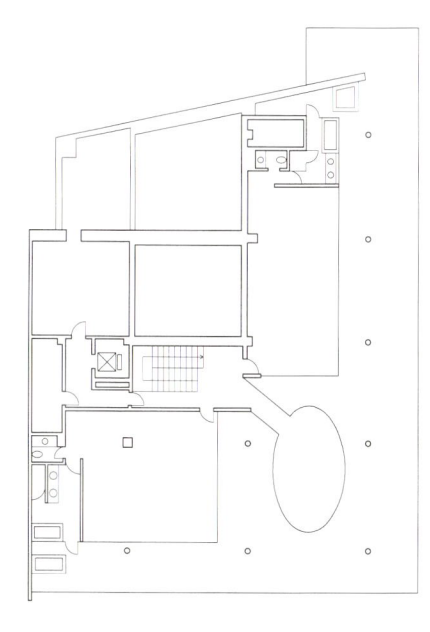

The house of Water and Glass 91

Kisho Kurokawa

1. Republic Plaza
1995

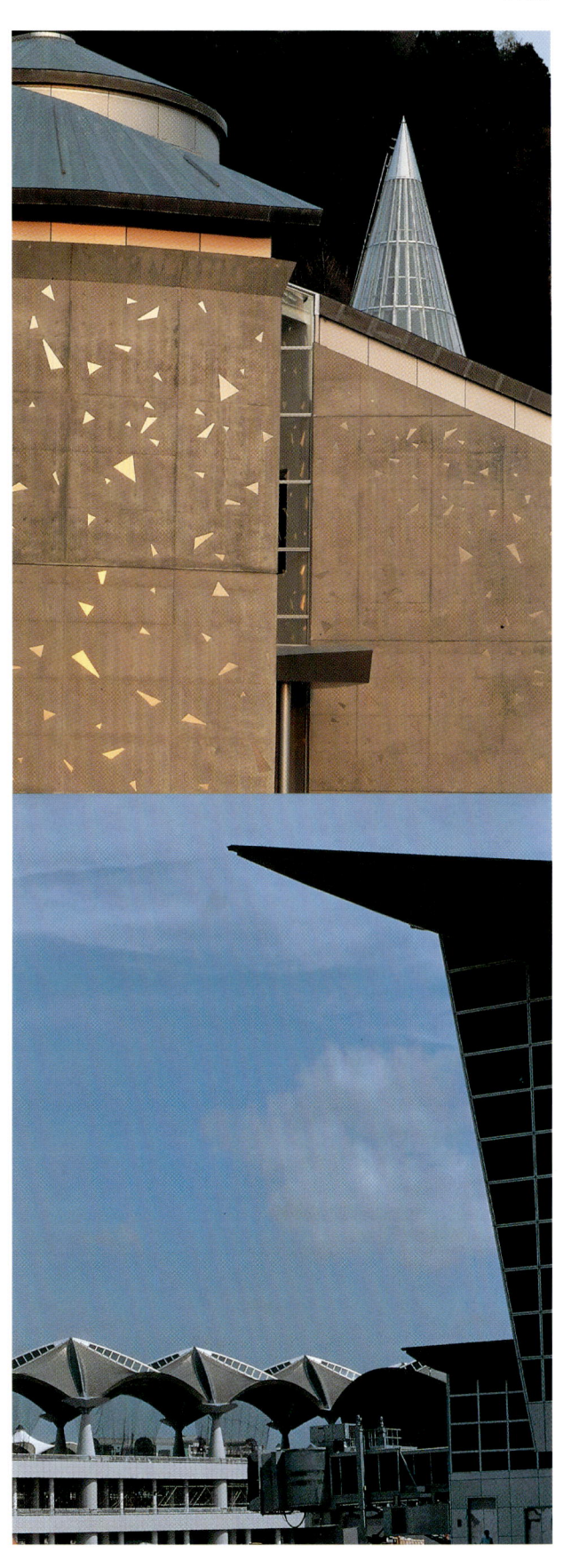

3. Shiga Kogen Roman Art Museum
1996

2. Melbourne Central
1991

4. Kuala Lumpur International Airport
1998

Wakayama Museum of Modern Art
1994

Kurokawa is a member of the generation of Japanese architects who formed part of the Metabolist movement in their youth and who now, in their mature works, are revising those theories. This makes it very interesting to compare the career of Kurokawa with those of Fumihiko Maki and Arata Isozaki, who also feature in this book. Of the three, perhaps it is Kurokawa who developed the most radical projects in the seventies. Their posterior work has seen Maki articulating his designs by the use of very concrete elements, while Isozaki has tried to integrate oriental and western traditions and Kurokawa has developed an undoubted capacity to resolve large scale projects by the use of simple forms.

In Kurokawa´s work, elements such as the cone or the semi-circular floor plan are constantly repeated in a way which means his architecture is composed on the basis of the juxtaposition of pure forms. For example, the cone is represented by the Gallery commemorating the expedition to the South Pole in Akita (1988), the hall of the Melbourne Central Skyscraper (1991), Lane Crawford Place shopping mall in Singapore (1993), Ehime Science Museum (1994), Shiga Kogen Roman Art Museum (1997) and the pillars of Kuala Lumpur Airport (1988). The cone is such an unusual element in modern architecture that this kind of repetition can be seen as a declaration of principles.

Kisho Kurokawa (Nagoya, 1934) studied architecture at the University of Kyoto and went on to obtain his doctor's degree at the University of Tokyo. When he was just 26, Kurokawa was one of the founder members of the Metabolist movement. The group's theories were formalized in projects such as Helix City Plan in 1961 (a great tower, which was never built, with a similar structure to that of DNA), the pavilion for Toshiba IHI at Expo'70 in Osaka, and the Sony office block and showroom, also in Osaka (1976).

His prestige was consolidated during the eighties, when he was awarded several international prizes and decorations and assigned major commissions; outstanding were a number of museums, such as Nagoya Art Museum (1987), Hiroshima Art Museum (1988), Wakayama Prefecture Museum (1990), Ehime Science Museum (1994), Fukui Art Museum (1997), and the Museum of Roman Art in Nagano (1997).

Kurokawa has also designed several skyscrapers such as Melbourne Central (1991) and Republic Plaza in Singapore (1995), but his largest-scale project is undoubtedly the new airport for Kuala Lumpur.

Wakayama Museum

- **Location:** Wakayama, Japan.
- **Construction:** 1994.
- **Architect:** Kisho Kurokawa.
- **Associates:** Tasuaki Tanaka, Akira Yokohama, Hiroshi Kanematsu, Kazunori Uchida, Masahiro Kamei, Seiki Iwasaki, Nobuo Abe, Yukio Yuoshida, Ichiro Tanaka, Naotake, Ueki, Iwao Miura.
- **Photographs:** Tomio Ohashi.

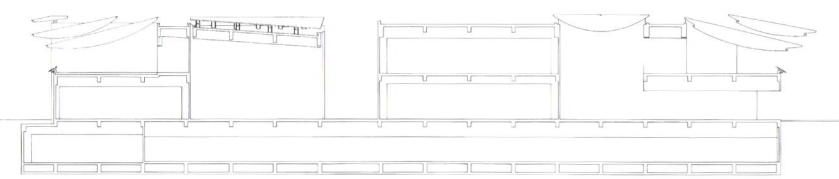

Kisho Kurokawa

Wakayama Museum of Modern Art

Ricardo Legorreta

1. Pershing Square
1994

2. Offices in Monterrey
1995

3. San Antonio Library
1995

4. South Chula Vista Library
1995

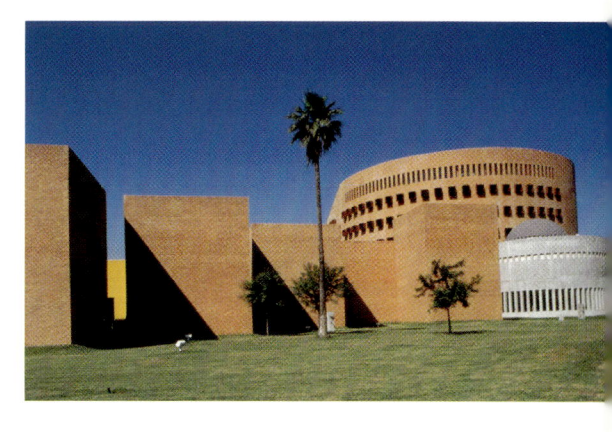

Monterrey Central Library 1994

Legorreta always credits José Villagrán as the architect who most influenced his own career. Yet for the simplicity of the forms he uses, the intensity of color, and his insistence on the vernacular, he is often associated with Luis Barragán. They do in fact have much in common, including some explicit references, shared interests, and a twenty-five year friendship, but although the architecture of Barragán and Legorreta start out from a common point, they go on to diverge, and follow quite different paths.

Barragán's work is introverted and sober, like the man himself. He controlled every aspect of his projects, even going so far as to construct models on a scale of 1:1. His is a singular, improbable, and profoundly mystic body of work. His spaces are conducive to spirituality, seclusion, quietude, and silence. It is difficult to imagine them crowded; there are no great halls, and almost none of them have more than two floors.

Legorreta, conversely, works within a team. Most of his works are for collective use -hotels, museums, offices, libraries- they are monumental, and urban in scale. He does not shirk the task of bringing people together, serving and representing them. His projects reinterpret much-visited places such as plazas and temples, and encourage activity.

Ricardo Legorreta, son of a family of bankers, was born in Mexico City in 1931. Between 1948 and 1952, he studied architecture at the Autonomous University of Mexico, at the same time working alongside José Villagrán García, one of the people responsible for introducing the modern movement into his country, and became a partner in the studio in 1955.

In 1963 he set up his own studio in Mexico City, and with the Automex Factory embarked on a long series of large-scale projects with social repercussions: the Camino Real Hotel in Mexico City, Conrad Hotel in Cancun, Monterrey Museum of Contemporary Art, Managua Cathedral, Pershing Square in Los Angeles, the La Solana estate for IBM next to Fort Worth airport in Texas, and Beirut Park Hotel in the Lebanon. Since 1969 he has also lectured intensively at the Autonomous University of Mexico, the Latin-American University, Harvard, University of Texas, and UCLA.

Monterrey Central Library

- **Location:** San Nicolás de los Ganza, Nuevo León, Mexico.
- **Construction:** 1994.
- **Client:** Autonomous University of Nuevo León.
- **Architect:** Legorreta Arquitectos.
- **Associates:** Armando Chávez, José Vigil (associate architects), DYS S.C. (structure), Tecno proyectos S.C. (installations), CB Consultores Asociados (lighting and contractor).
- **Photographs:** Lourdes Legorreta.

From the very beginning, the idea was to make the library blend in with its surroundings by integrating its volumetric composition into the natural environment. From the outside, the building stands out for its roundness and the simplicity of the geometric engagement, taking its place harmoniously in the surrounding park land, despite its size. Just two materials are used for the outer walls: brick for the imposing cylinder, in perfect conjunction with the bare concrete of all the other volumes, except the tower and entrance corridor which are also of plain masonry.

Traditional Mexican architectonic features are picked up in absolutely contemporary form. The flashes of intense color and the filtering of light through courtyards and latticework are reminiscent of the country's popular forms of architecture; it is the essence that is worked in here, with references to context; adapted rather than borrowed literally.

Ricardo Legorreta

Monterrey Central Library

Mark Mack

1. Napa Valley House
1983

2. Knipschild House
1985

3. House in Sausalito
1987

*Stremmel House
1995*

The use of color in the works of this Austrian architect is a decisive factor in the image of his projects (the legacy of the Mexican architect Barragán, the subject of an exhibition he worked on, upon his arrival in the USA in 1973); with it, he has delighted many clients in Los Angeles, where a number of his houses have been built. His first works were simple-lined houses, with the full backing of modern architecture, which he adapted to the conditions of the modern American lifestyle. With Summers House (Santa Monica, 1989-1991), he started to apply himself with greater versatility to the external composition of the buildings, taking a free hand with bright colors and elements unrelated to strictly tectonic principles (such as sequences of water). His chromatic treatment of large surfaces shows his skill in exploiting the use of different materials, which we notice in the details of his homes and in his furniture designs. Moving beyond California, other housing commissions show that the impact of color continues to characterize his work, independently of where it is located.

Mark Mack (1949) graduated from the Vienna Academy of Fine Arts (1973). At the time, he was working for Steiger & Partners and Hans Hollein. He then moved to the States, which is where most of his work has been produced. Since 1990, he has lived in California. When he arrived in New York in 1973, he worked with Emilio Ambasz on an exhibition about Luis Barragán. His first intervention in California was the project for ten houses in different parts of the city (1977-1978), which presented different visions of how to live in harmony with nature. His commissions started to change scale after the competition he entered, along with other internationally renowned studios, for the new Getty Center in Los Angeles (which was ultimately won by Richard Meier); he was then awarded the remodeling of the Getty Center for the History of Art and Humanities in Santa Monica (California, 1984-1985).

In one of his home designs (Whitney House, Los Angeles, California, 1986-1988, 1990), he had to restructure three wings designed by Gehry, respecting their original volumes and joining them by the use of roofs and color alone. One of his most famous housing blocks is Nexus (1989-1991), designed for the Japanese city of Fukuoka, where there are also blocks by Steven Holl, Rem Koolhaas, Osamu Ishiyama, Christian de Portzamparc, and Oscar Tusquets.

Stremmel House

- **Location:** Reno, Nevada, USA.
- **Construction:** 1994.
- **Architect:** Mark Mack.
- **Photographs:** Undine Pröhl.

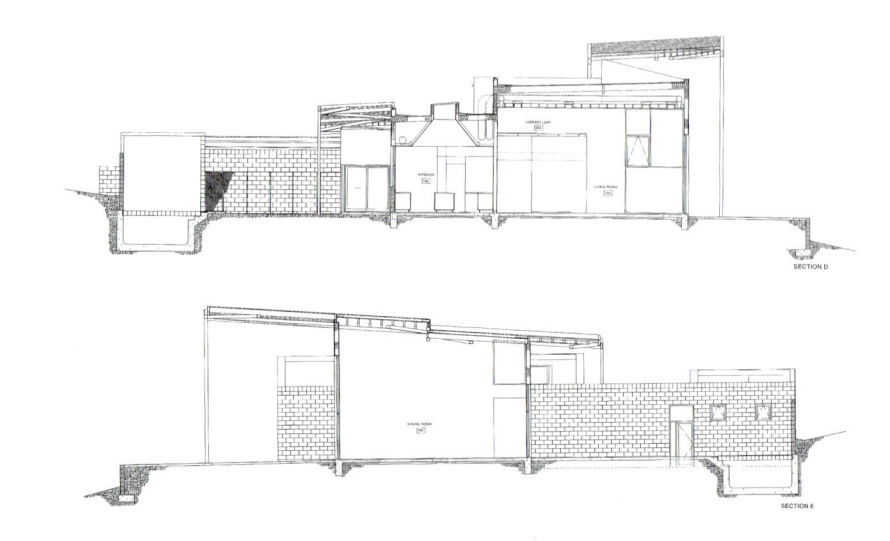

In a way, Stremmel House reproduces the organizational scheme of the old houses built around courtyards, their volumes surrounding a central, empty space containing a swimming pool or pond. The need to delineate the limits of intervention in the face of the immensity of the desert led him to place the house on a concrete platform. Mack was aware that creating a microcosm that is different to the predominant aridity is a difficult task, and therefore concentrated habitable space within specific limits. Inside this parallelepiped of air he differentiates and joins up volumes, paying attention to their interconnection and creating a floating, fluid space, which is both indoors and outdoors and ultimately makes sense of the overall project.

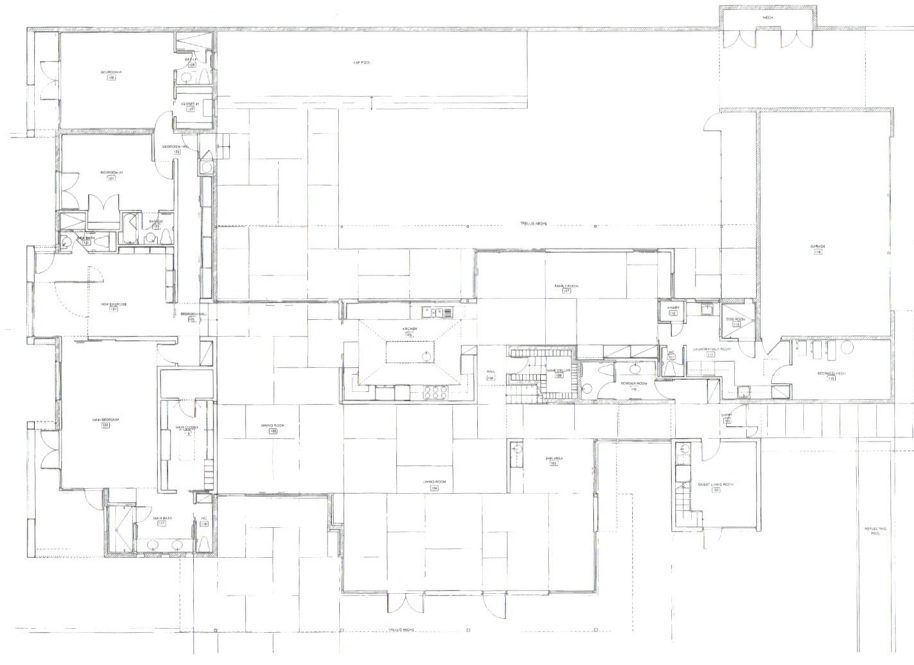

102 *Mark Mack*

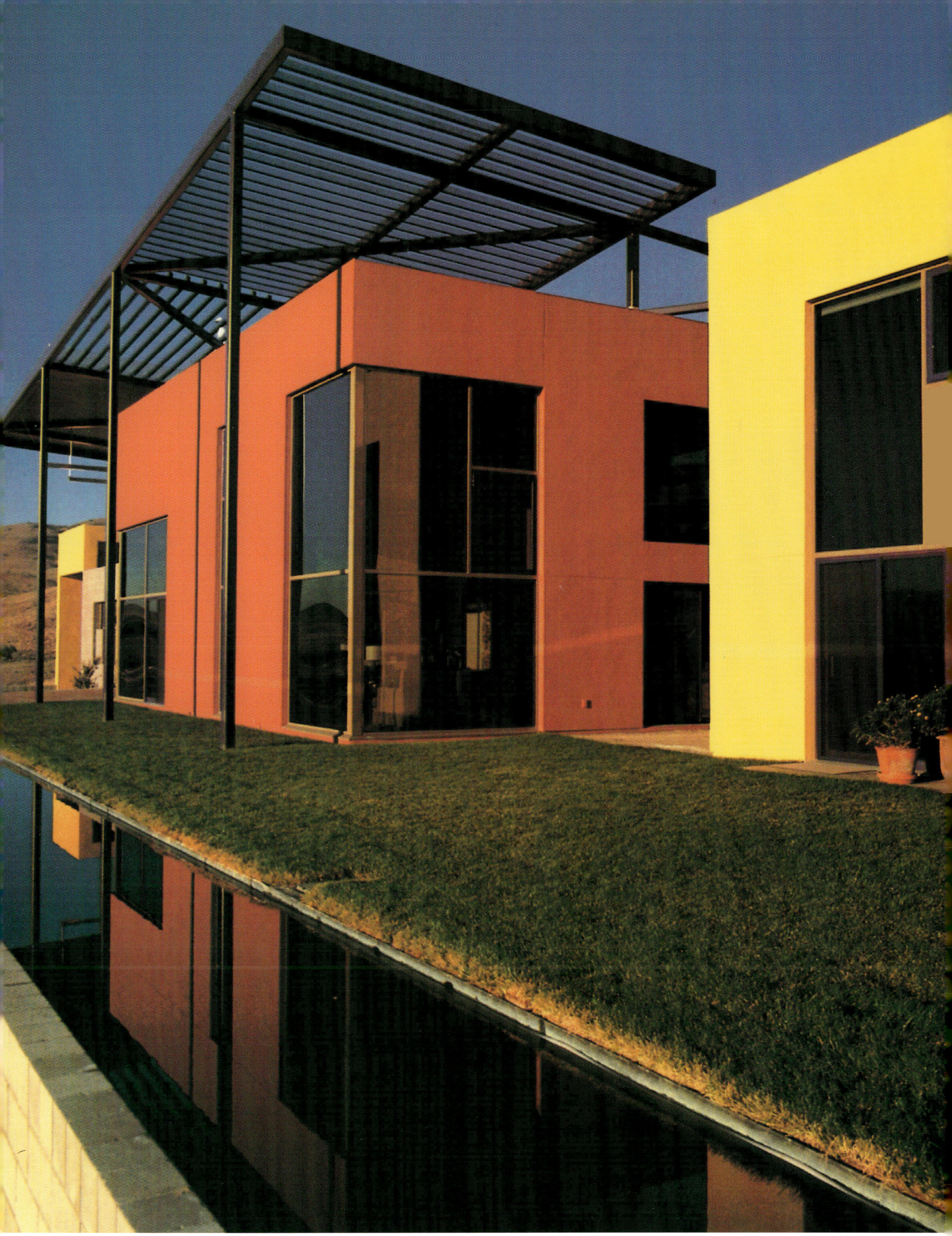

… Fumihiko Maki

1. Fujisawa Stadium
1984

2. SPIRAL Building
1985

3. Tokyo Metropolitan Gymnasium
1990

Tokyo Church
1995

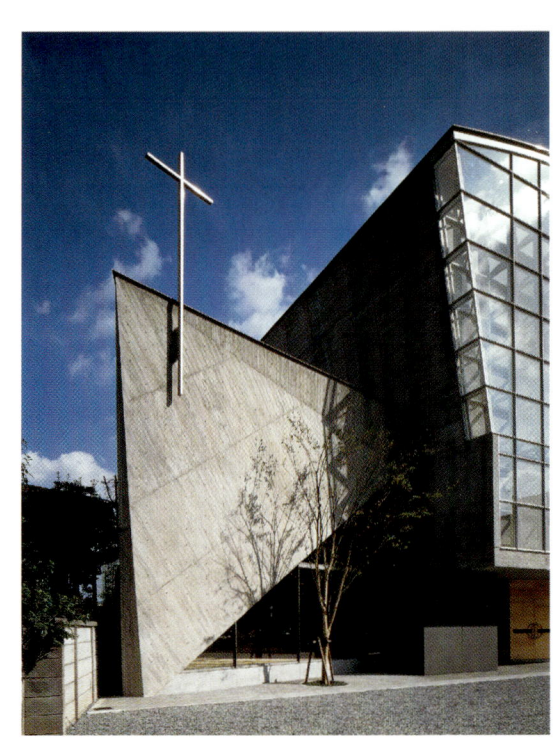

Kaze-no-Oka Crematorium 1997

Maki's architecture is underlain by the vital importance of his research into the collective forms of the sixties. At that time, he formed part of the Metabolist movement, but without defending its futuristic-looking megastructures. Maki set forward an idea he called "Group-form", a methodology to generate the city by joining up small parts. In particular, Maki confessed that, at the time, he was very much influenced by his visit to Mediterranean towns on a trip he made in 1959, which inspired a completely different image from the visionary proposals of Kiyonaro Kikutake, for instance.

His way of working from the small to the large permeates all of his later work. Even in buildings that are more difficult to adapt to this methodology, such as gymnasiums, swimming pools, and large sports centers, Maki has developed the project from the inside out. Before defining the form, Maki concentrates on the space, studying the program and itineraries. During this process, the building is just a nebula which crystallizes when the inner space is finally defined.

After studying architecture in his native city, Fumihiko Maki (Tokyo, 1928) moved to the United States to complete his studies at the Cranbrook Academy of Art and at Harvard. He worked in the studios of Skidmore, Owings & Merrill (S.O.M.) and Josep Lluìs Sert (who had been his lecturer at Harvard). Maki was a founder member of the Metabolist group. He took part in the World Design Conference held in Tokyo in 1960.

In 1965, he set up Maki & Associates in Tokyo and since then has produced such outstanding works as the Sports Center in the Prefecture of Osaka (1972), Fujisawa Municipal Gymnasium in Kanawa (1984), the SPIRAL building in Tokyo (1985), the Kyoto Museum of Modern Art (1986), Tokyo Metropolitan Gymnasium (1990), the Yerba Buena Gardens Art Center in downtown San Francisco (1993), the Church of Christ in the Tomigaya district (1995), and the Kaze-no-Oka Crematorium (1997). At the same time, from 1966 to 1992, Maki was involved in the construction of the Daikan-Yama complex in Tokyo, a whole district of low-rise residential buildings and business premises, with small-scale public spaces. In 1993, Maki was awarded the Pritzker Prize for his work as a whole.

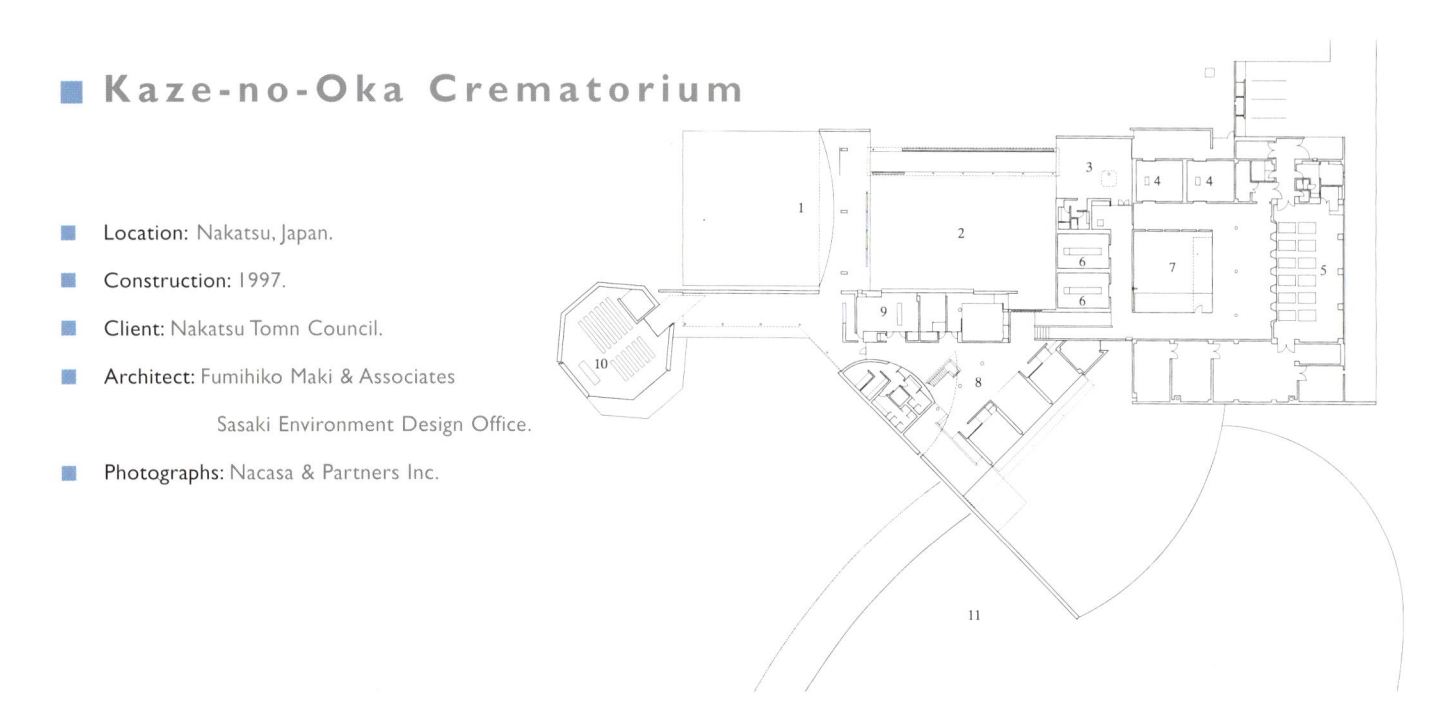

Kaze-no-Oka Crematorium

- Location: Nakatsu, Japan.
- Construction: 1997.
- Client: Nakatsu Tomn Council.
- Architect: Fumihiko Maki & Associates
  Sasaki Environment Design Office.
- Photographs: Nacasa & Partners Inc.

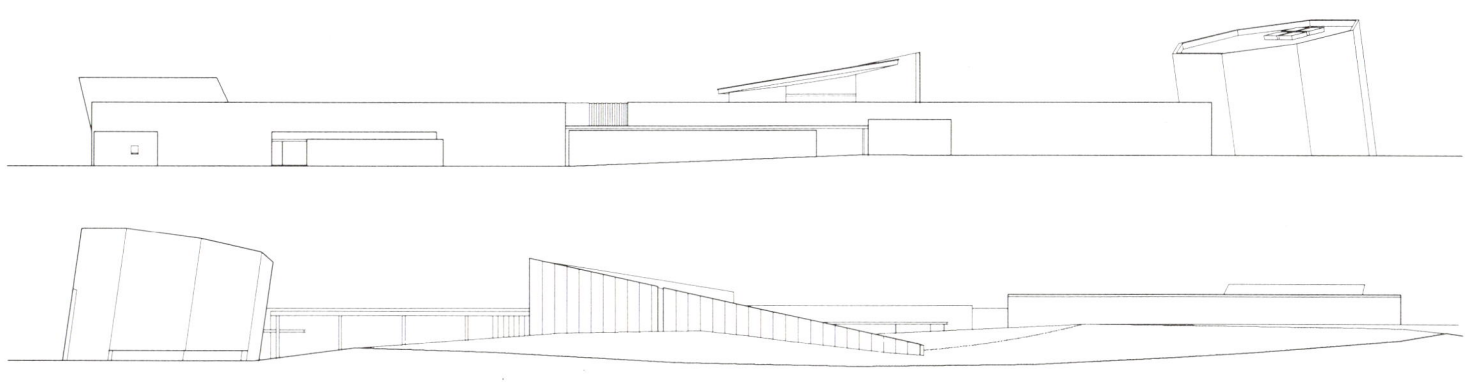

Architectural approaches and landscaping instruments are combined throughout the grounds, so that architecture becomes a device for the construction of a landscape, and the landscape constantly makes use of architectural instruments. The strategy applied to the park highlights changes in paving, trees, topographical workings of great geometric rigidity, straight-lined paths, etc. The notion of vertical movement is present throughout: in the building, it is expressed through the openings; in the park, through the rise and fall of the ground, culminating at the lowest point in the center of the ellipse, a point where the whole experience appears to come to a close. At the same time, the sloping volume of the chapel seems to question this fundamental sense of verticality, to make architecture renounce its most intrinsic qualities.

Kaze-no-Oka Crematorium

Mecanoo

1. Housing in Rotterdam
1985

2. House with studio
1991

3. The Economics Faculty, Utrecht
1995

Housing in Maastricht 1994

The inexhaustibility of the modern movement is one of the founding principles of the architecture of the Mecanoo group. For them, the history of architecture is a vast array of formal and functional models which are there to be used, not questioned. To some extent, we could say that the architecture of Mecanoo is "postmodernist" in that it turns to models from the past to emphasize present-day architecture. It is this re-use that suggests the virtuosity of the team: once the direction of the architectonic solution has been decided, the project moves on to a study of construction methods and materials, with particular attention to detail. This has led the team to explore the paths of standardization, coming up with designs based on modulations which make their projects simpler and more flexible, making them particularly distinctive. Some of their works are communal family housing units which, when touched by the team's planning logic, become individual entities which group together horizontally or vertically, as we can see in the project in Stuttgart. In one of their more recent works, the restoration of a historic building, they opted for contrast in the form of a large glazed hall shaped like a whale, suspended in the inner courtyard and set over the original building; the role of the structure in this solution is fundamental in the effect produced inside the building.

Henk Döll (1956), Erick Van Egeraat (1956), Francine Houben (1955), and Chris de Weijer (1956) studied at the University of Delft (Holland). One of their first well-known projects was the winning entry in a competition to construct a block of houses in Rotterdam (Kruisplein, 1980-1985), for this purpose they formed the team known as Mecanoo. The use of modern architecture as a model has been present since their earliest projects. In some, they remind us directly of the grand masters, as in the case of the housing units in the port of Rotterdam (Hillekop, 1985-1989), where we recognize the Aalto of Bremen's towers. Particularly outstanding among their home proposals are the "green" homes for the International Horticulture Exhibition. This project displays Mecanoo's way of thinking, comprising a housing complex made up of the grouping of individual cells.

Housing in Maastricht

- **Location:** Herdenkingsplein, Holland.
- **Construction:** 1994.
- **Architects:** Mecanoo.
- **Client:** Maastricht City Council.
- **Construction company:** Bouwmaatschappij Keulen, Geleen.
- **Associates:** ABT technical consultants, Delft.
- **Photograph:** Christian Richters.

It was the approach to their project via the plaza that led to the distinctive treatment of its facade: "Rather than allowing it to become a simple collection of separate homes, we wanted something communal which would provide a shared basis for the homes and vice versa." The houses are situated behind a screen of varnished cedar which conceals the living rooms, balconies, and the galleries leading to each individual unit from community staircases, laid out around the outer portico. This gallery connects the two blocks in which the project was finally structured, creating an illusion of a single facade for what are, in fact, independent blocks.

Mecanoo

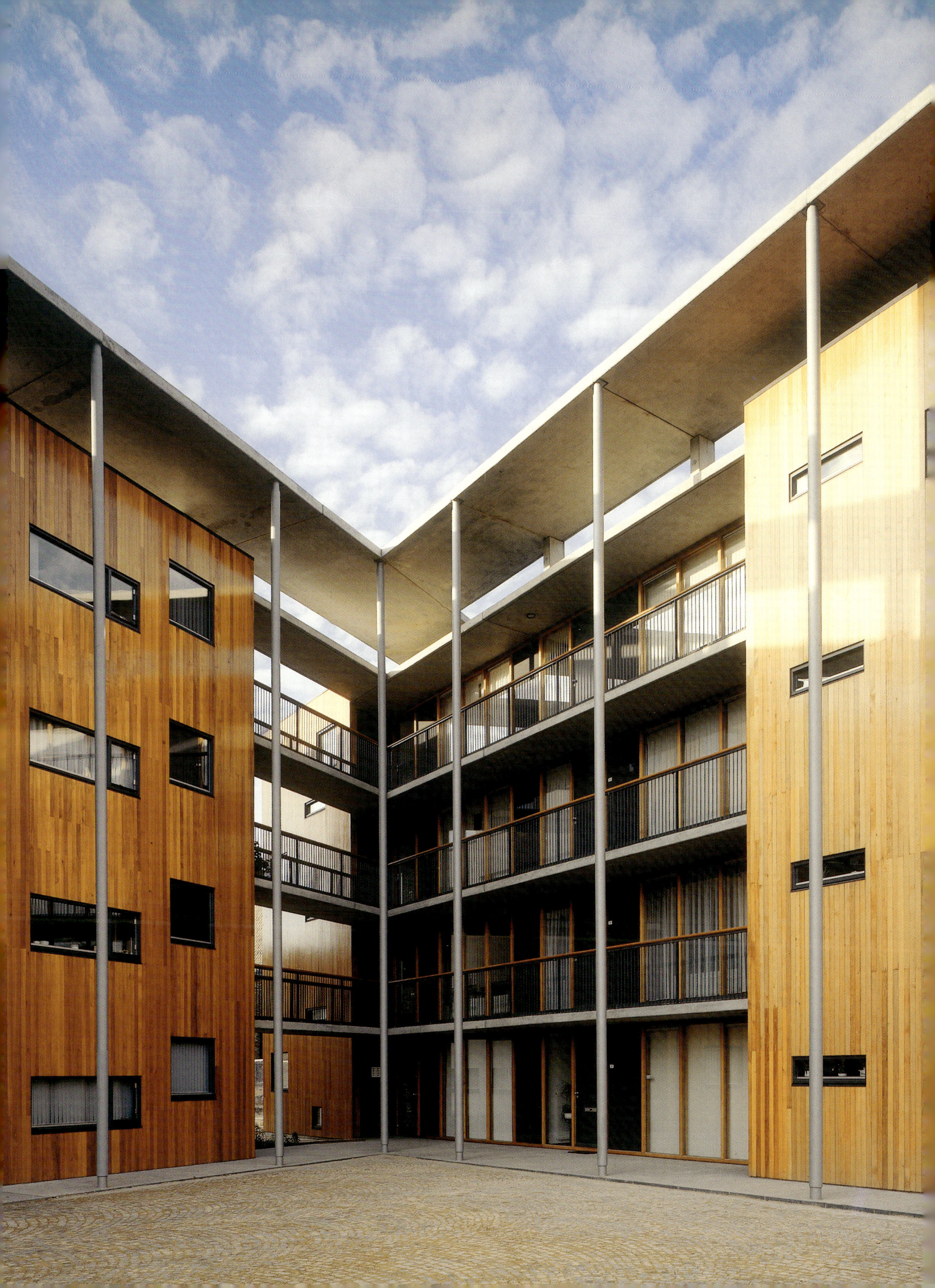

Richard Meier

1. Ackersberg House
1986

2. Grotta House
1989

3. Bridgeport Center
1989

4. Westchester Country House
1986

Barcelona Museum of Contemporary Art 1996

The formal evolution leading from Smith House (1965) to any of Richard Meier's recent projects such as the Getty Center (1984-1997) is practically non-existent. His career throughout these thirty years is unusually coherent, not just for architecture but for any activity.

To a large extent this is due to the fact that his emergence into the world of architecture was surprisingly successful for a thirty-year-old. Shortly after completing work on Smith House, he joined Eisenman, Hejduk, Graves, and Gwathmey for the exhibition Five Architects at the MOMA. From this moment on, they became known as the Whites, and many reviews of the group appeared in leading international publications. Meier's work has been seen as an American reworking of the European architecture of the thirties, especially that of Le Corbusier. The use of a particular language is essential to a definition of his projects. This involves not just the color white, but also the railings, curved walls, rectangular porticoes, etc.

Shortly after finishing his architecture studies at Cornell University, Richard Meier (Newak, 1934) started to teach at the Pratt Institute, and later at the Cooper Union and Yale. In 1965 he set up his own studio in New York and became part of the group Five Architects. His early works -mainly country houses- have been well publicized: Smith House (1965), Hoffman House (1966), Saltzman House (1969), the house in Old Westbury (1969) and the famous Douglas House (1971), set in a conifer forest beside Lake Michigan. In 1970, he also started to work on public buildings such as the Athenaeum in New Harmony (Indiana, 1979) and, in the eighties, to carry out projects in Europe, especially after the success of his Museum of Decorative Arts in Frankfurt (1985). In 1986, Meier was awarded the Pritzker Prize and the commission to build the pharaonic project of the Getty Center in Los Angeles, which was completed in 1997.

Barcelona Museum of Contemporary Art

Barcelona Museum of Contemporary Art

- **Location:** Barcelona, Spain.
- **Construction:** 1996.
- **Architect:** Richard Meier.
- **Associates:** Richard Meier, Thomas Phifer (design team); Renny Logan, Alfonso Pérez (project); Fernando Ramos, Isabel Bachs (associates); Obiols, Brufau, Moya, Arquitectos (structure); Francesc Labastida (installations); Fischer, Marantz, Renfro & Stone (lighting).
- **Photographs:** Eugeni Pons.

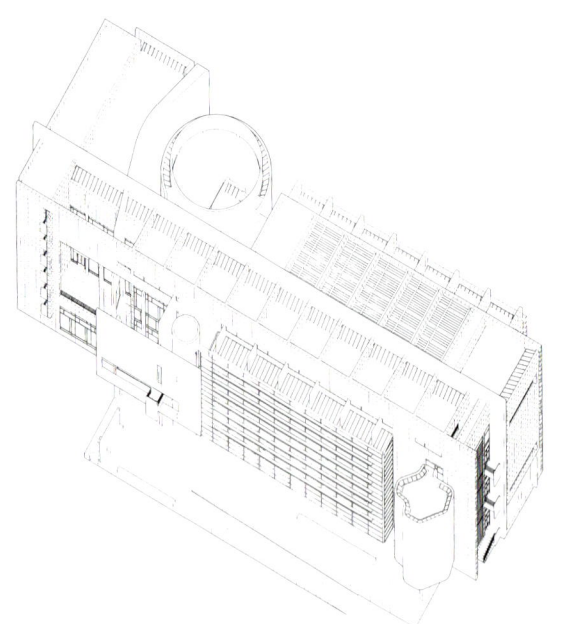

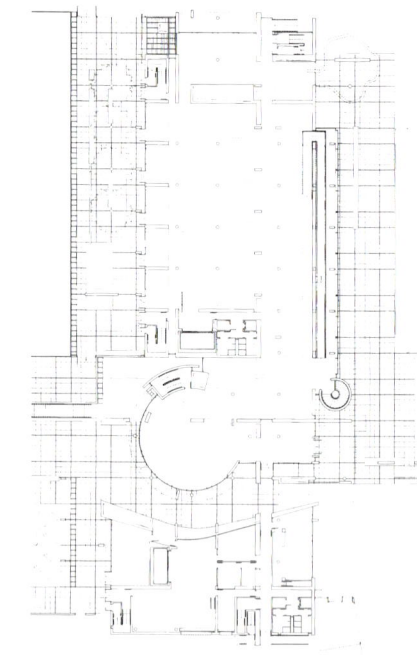

The Barcelona Museum of Contemporary Art is completely representative of Meier's characteristic plastic language, based on a clear rationalism which combines straight and curved lines, to set up a harmonious dialogue between the inside spaces and the light drawn in via great galleries and glazed expanses.

114 *Richard Meier*

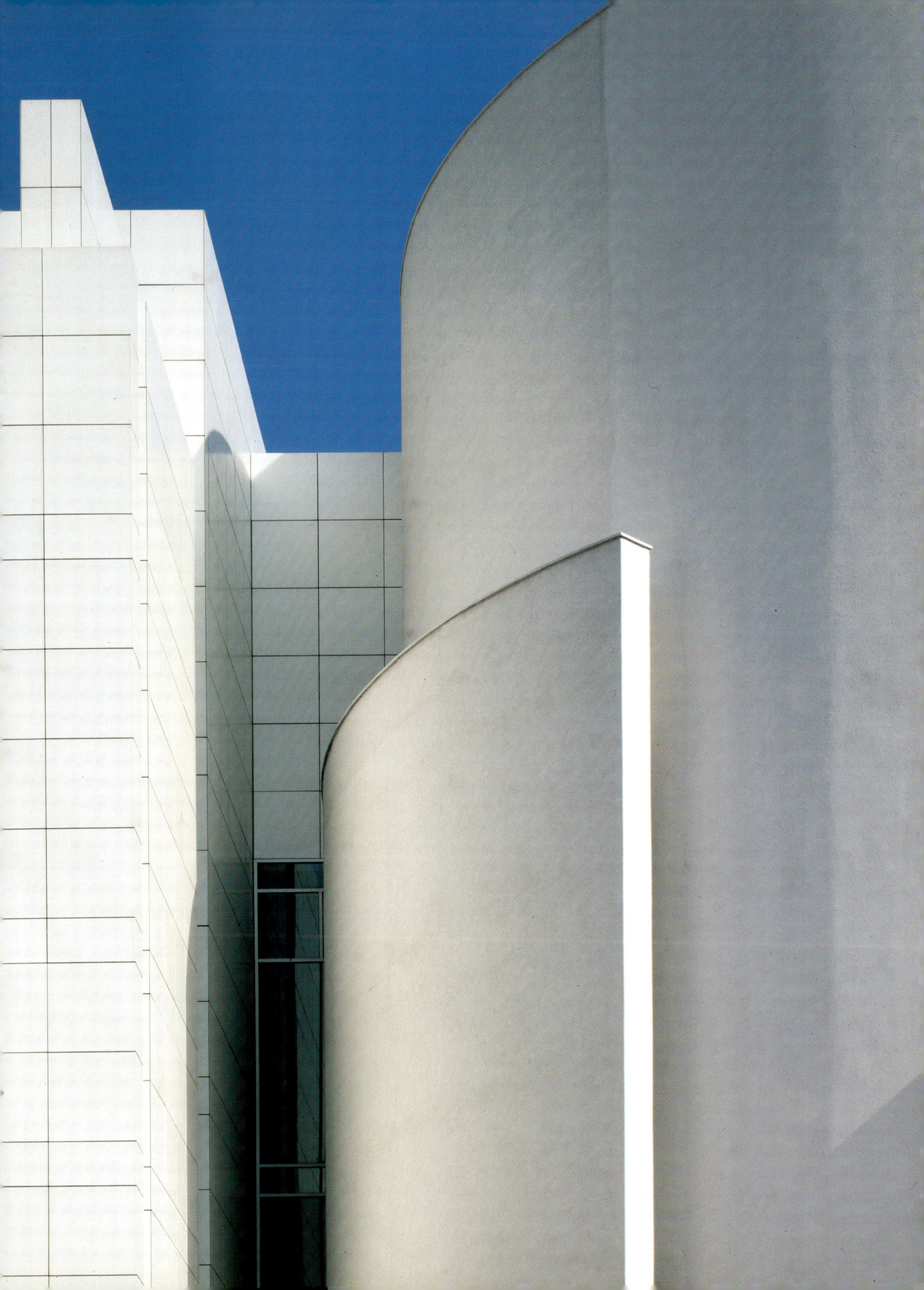

Enric Miralles

1. Huesca Sports Center
   1994

2. Archery Installations
   1992

3. Plaza in Parets
   1983

Mercaders House 1994

Enric Miralles' work started to become known at a time when the word deconstructivism was on everyone's lips, which explains why he was mistakenly included in this trend. Nonetheless, his work is inspired by Le Corbusier (drawings as well as built work), the facility of Gaudì and Jujol to reinterpret natural forms, and the extraordinary part played by topography in the project.

Miralles' buildings frequently start out from metaphors, images, or ideas which have little to do with architecture, or are planned as buildings which are not completely finished. Perhaps this is why they blend in so perfectly with their surroundings.

Since his split with Carme Pinós, his projects have lost some of the restraint and lyricism that works such as Igualada Cemetery possessed in abundance. His latest works are more spectacular and inspired, but also less poetic.

This may be due in part to the increasing protagonism of metal and wood replacing concrete as the main construction materials in his work.

Enric Miralles (Barcelona, 1955) studied architecture in the city of his birth, graduating in 1978. From 1973 to 1984, he worked in association with the studio of Albert Viaplana and Helio Piñón. In 1983, together with Carme Pinós, he set up a studio in Barcelona.

Despite having little built work to their names the plaza in Parets (1983), La Llauna School in Badalona (1986) by the end of the eighties, Miralles and PinÛs were the object of international admiration for their competition entries and projects for works still under construction Igualada Cemetery (1991), the Archery Facilities (1992), and Els Hostalets Cultural Center (1993). This early success was due to a large extent to the beauty of their designs and the quality of their models.

In the early nineties, Miralles split from Pinós and went into partnership with Benedetta Tagliabue. At this time, he completed some large-scale projects such as the Sports Center in Huesca (1994) and Alicante Gymnastics Center (1995). He also started work on projects in Japan and Germany. Enric Miralles combines his professional practise with lecturing at several universities.

Mercaders House

The project involved renovating a building in Barcelona's old town as a home for these two architects.

- Location: Barcelona, Spain.
- Construction: 1994.
- Architects: Enric Miralles, Benedetta Tagliabue.
- Associates: R. Brufau (structure), Jardineria Moix (landscaping), Tierra y Mar (construction company).
- Photographs: Eugeni Pons.

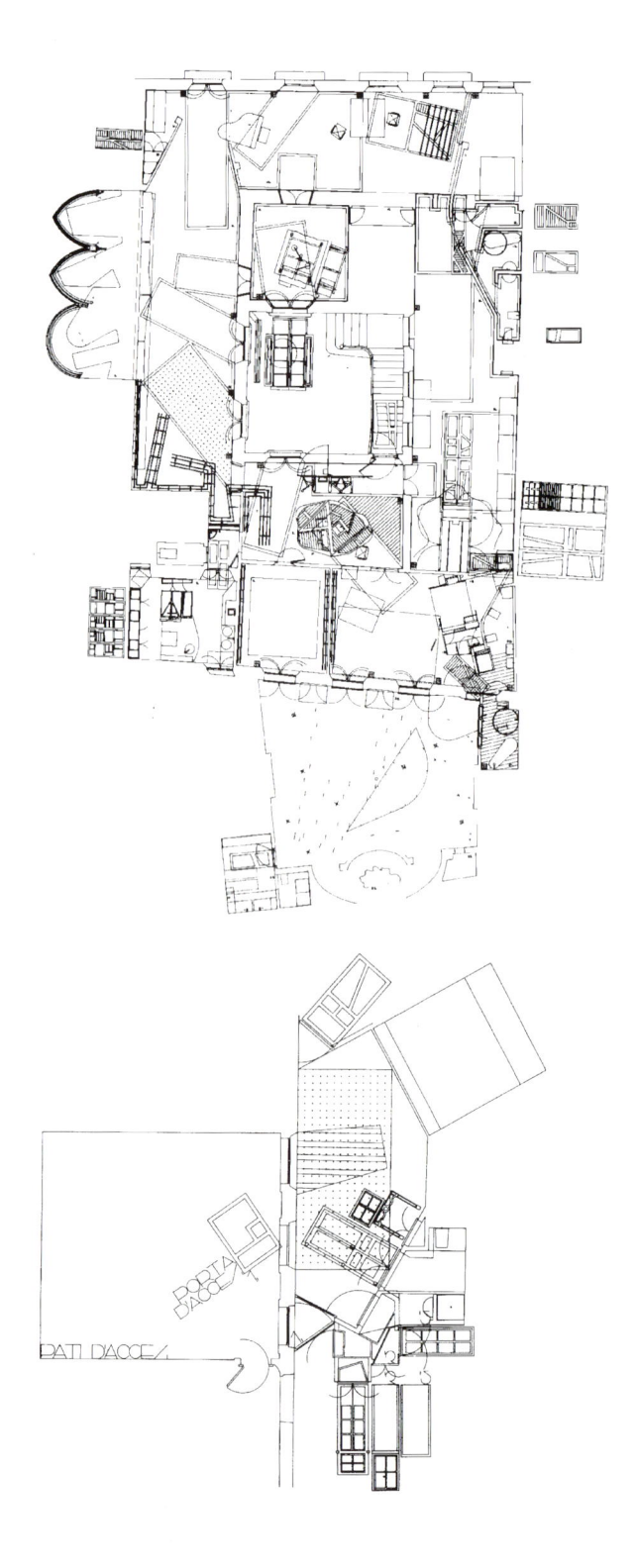

118 *Enric Miralles*

Mercaders House 119

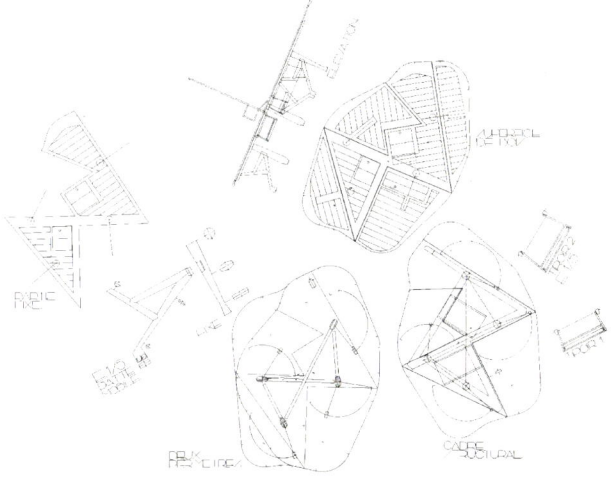

Rafael Moneo

1. Atocha Station
1988

2. L'Illa Diagonal
1994

Stockholm Museum of Modern Art
1998

More than a designer, Rafael Moneo is a scholar of architecture. Whether it is the influence of his lecturing work, or due to his interest in history, each of his projects is a theme for reflection on the city, on topography, on classical language, or traditional typologies.

It is often said that none of Moneo's buildings is like another. The Navarrese architect is mistrusting of idiosyncrasies of style, "My aim is to avoid falling into the trap of linguistic error, that feeling we often get when we look at examples of recent architecture which have been destroyed in the attempt to establish paradigms, while ignoring the real problems."

As a result, people often label Moneo as an eclectic architect who, rather than imposing his work on the context, seeks to integrate his project in it, adopting many aspects of the architectural context in which his works are set. Yet this eclecticism does not translate as formal caprice: his buildings are rigorously abstract, as his elegant progress through postmodernism and deconstructivism goes to show.

After graduating from the Madrid School of Architecture, Rafael Moneo Vallés (Tudela, 1937) worked in association with Sáenz de Oiza (1958-1961) and Jørn Utzon (1961-1962). Since the mid-sixties, Moneo has lectured extensively in Madrid, Barcelona, Lausanne, Princeton, and Harvard, where he was dean of the design school in the early nineties.

Since 1970, Rafael Moneo has carried out major commissions such as the head office of Bankinter in Madrid (1976), Logroño City Hall (1981), the celebrated Museum of Roman Art in Merida (1986), the head office of Previsión Española in Seville (1988), the Bank of Spain main branch in Jaen (1988), San Pablo Airport in Seville (1991), Atocha Station in Madrid (1992) and the shopping mall L'Illa Diagonal in Barcelona (1993).

Prizes (including the Pritzker Prize), fame, and international commissions started to come in the nineties. During this period he has designed several museums: the Thyssen-Bornemisza in Madrid (1992), the head office of the Pilar and Joan Miró Foundation in Palma (1993), the Davis Museum in Massachusetts (1993), and the Museum of Modern Art in Stockholm (1998).

Stockholm Museum of Modern Art **121**

The Stockholm
Museum of Modern Art

- Location: Stockholm, Sweden.
- Construction: 1998.
- Client: Swedish National Board of Public Works.
- Architect: Rafael Moneo.
- Associates: Michael Bischoff, Robert Robinowitz, Lucho Marcial.
- Photographs: WENZEL.

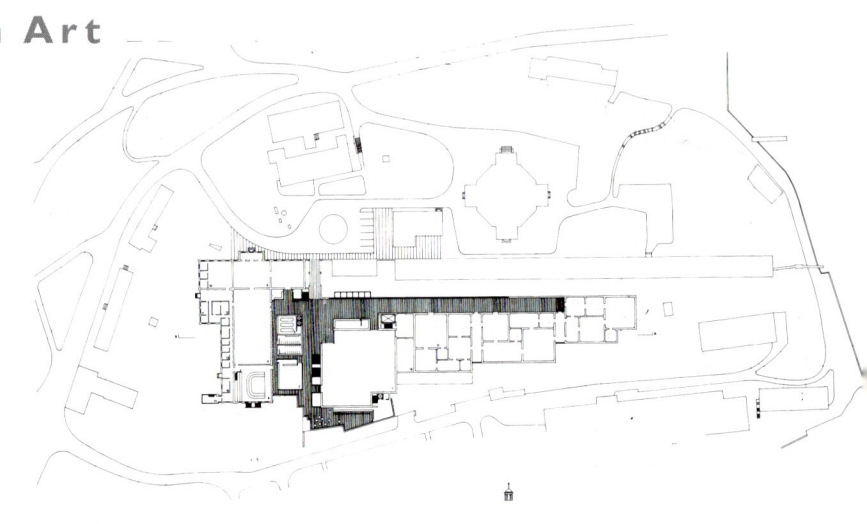

The project is based on a typological study of the exhibition galleries. Moneo decided to build four-square galleries with pyramidal roofs which finish in a central skylight. Each gallery has its own individual roof. Another of the museum's major features is the great glass-covered terrace of the cafeteria.

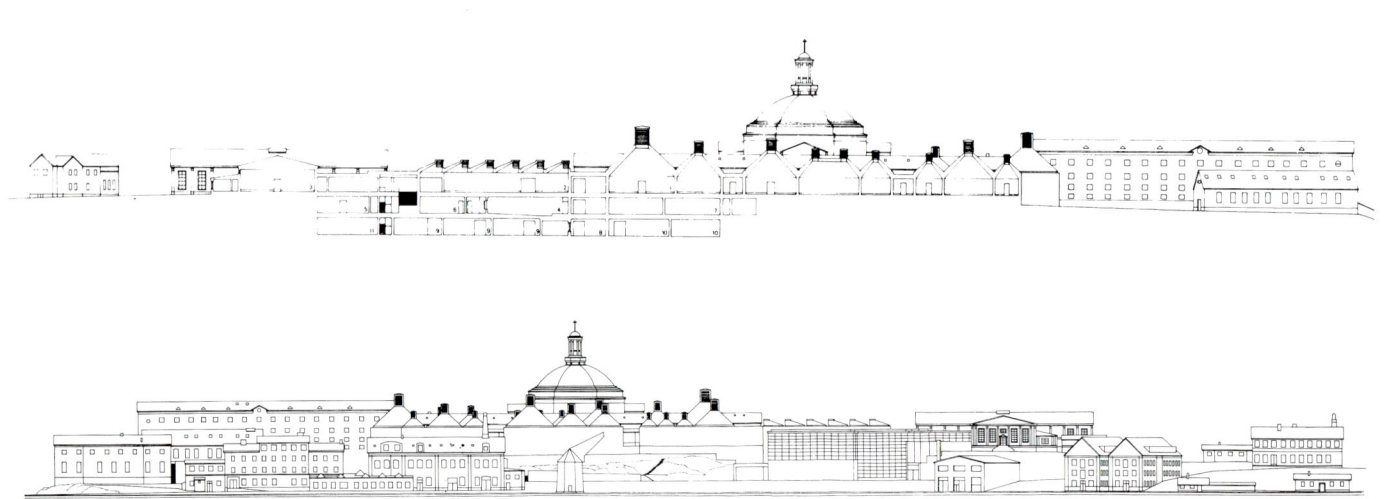

122 *Rafael Moneo*

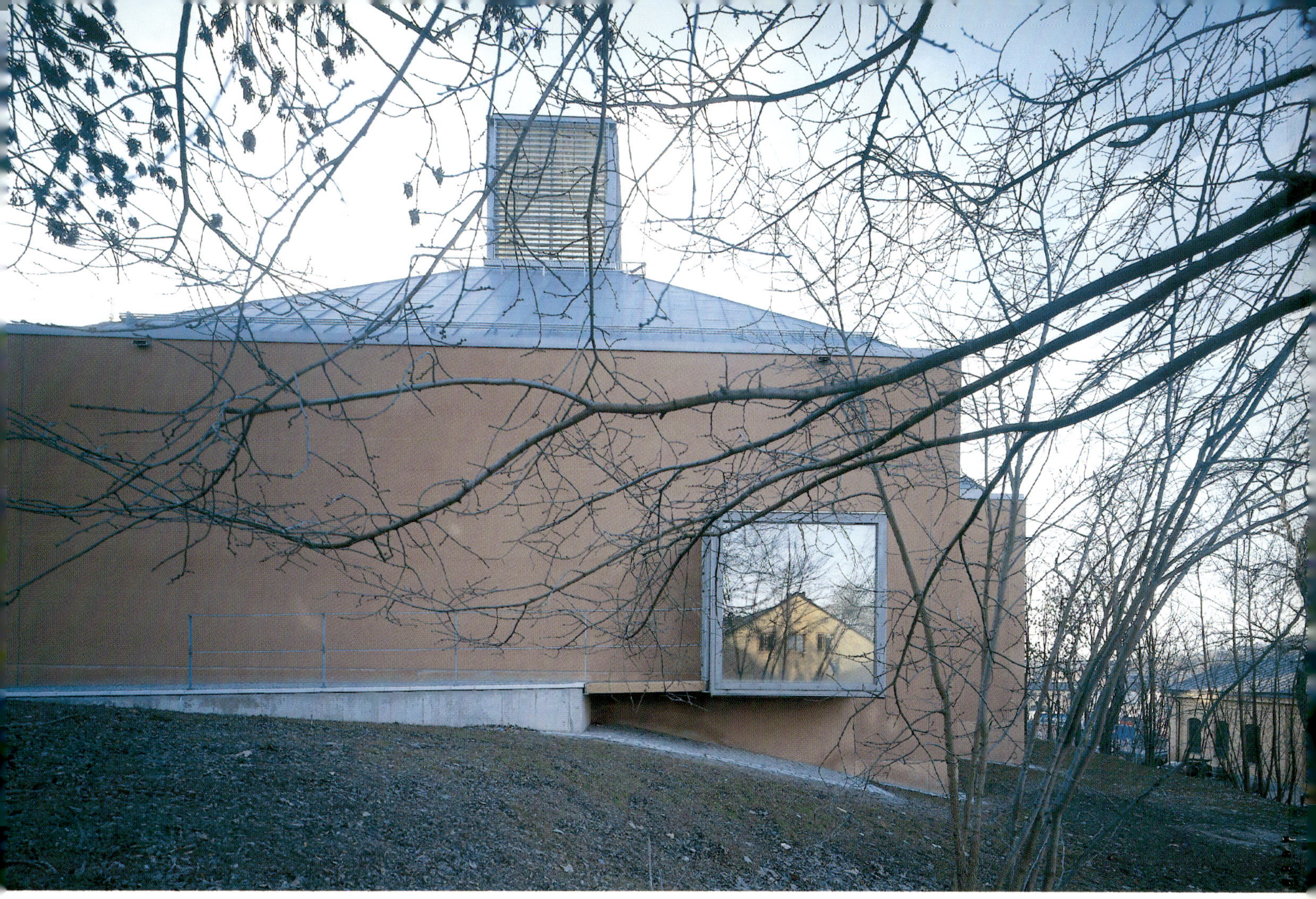

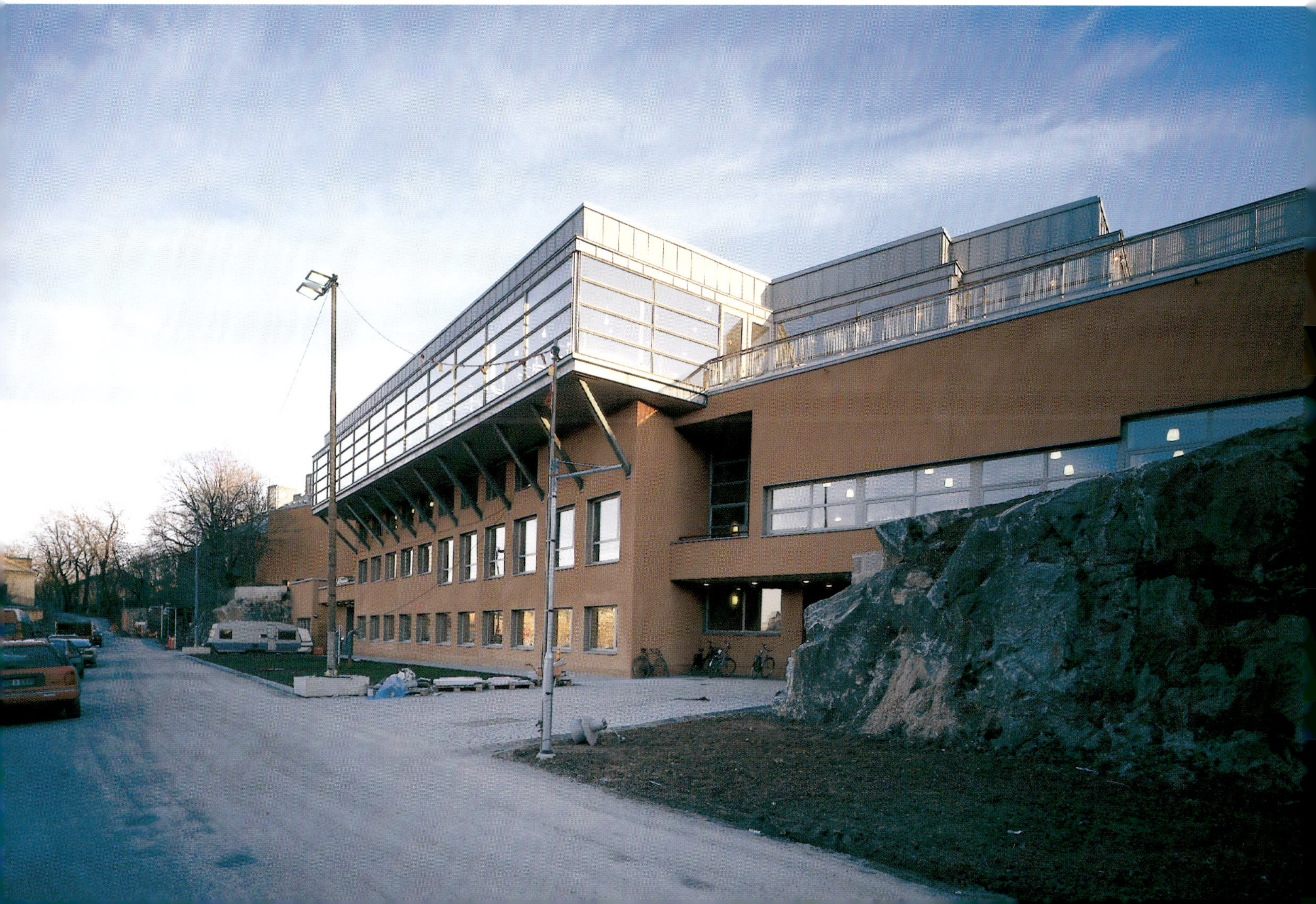

Morphosis

1. *House in Hermosa Beach*
   1990

2. *Golf club in Chiba*
   1991

*Blades House
1996*

Over and above any prevailing fashions, it is the "changes" in architecture as a discipline that are reflected in the research of this Californian team. Their way of working reveals their concern with the theme of architecture as such: the design process is never seen to be finished—they constantly go back to it to rework sketches and models, even once the project is finished. This means that every new proposal is seen as a step forward in the team's theoretical reflections. This process could lead to abstraction, but even so, their buildings make concessions enough to the context without needing to compromise their conceptual idea.

They are often included in the Frank Gehry tradition, yet while this architect seems to have a taste for the articulation of increasingly complex volumes, Morphosis' volumetric results are the outcome of more elementary geometry, which also lead to structural proposals. On the Californian scene, the architecture of Morphosis refuses to fall in with a "flavor-of-the-month" philosophy, despite running the risk of being labeled abstract and chaotic, like any counter-trend.

Morphosis was set up by Tom Mayne (a 1968 graduate) and Michael Rotondi, who left the team in around 1991. Its first well-known works were determined by existing structures: in 1986, the Kate Mantilini Restaurant (Beverly Hills), and the CCC (Comprehensive Cancer Center, Los Angeles) in 1987. In 1990 they designed Crawford House in California, where they aimed to harmonize the architecture with its surroundings, ignoring the closed typology of traditional houses. When they were well known in the States, they received a commission from Japan for a golf club in Chiba (1991), where they attempted to go one step further in asserting their relationship with the environment. Also in 1991, they restructured a building in Los Angeles (Salick Offices), where they managed to create a completely new image for the old building by means of a formal and programmatic change. In 1993 they were commissioned to design "a non-traditional home" in California (Blades House), where the limits between indoors-outdoors and even of space are completely merged in an almost sculptural container. They have taken part in many international competitions, such as the one for the Higashi-Azabu office block (Tokyo, 1989), the urban design proposal for Potsdamer Platz in Berlin (1990) and Nara Convention Center (Japan, 1992).

Blades House

- Location: Santa Barbara, California, USA
- Construction: 1996
- Client: the Blades family
- Architect: Morphosis
- Photographs: Kim Zwarts

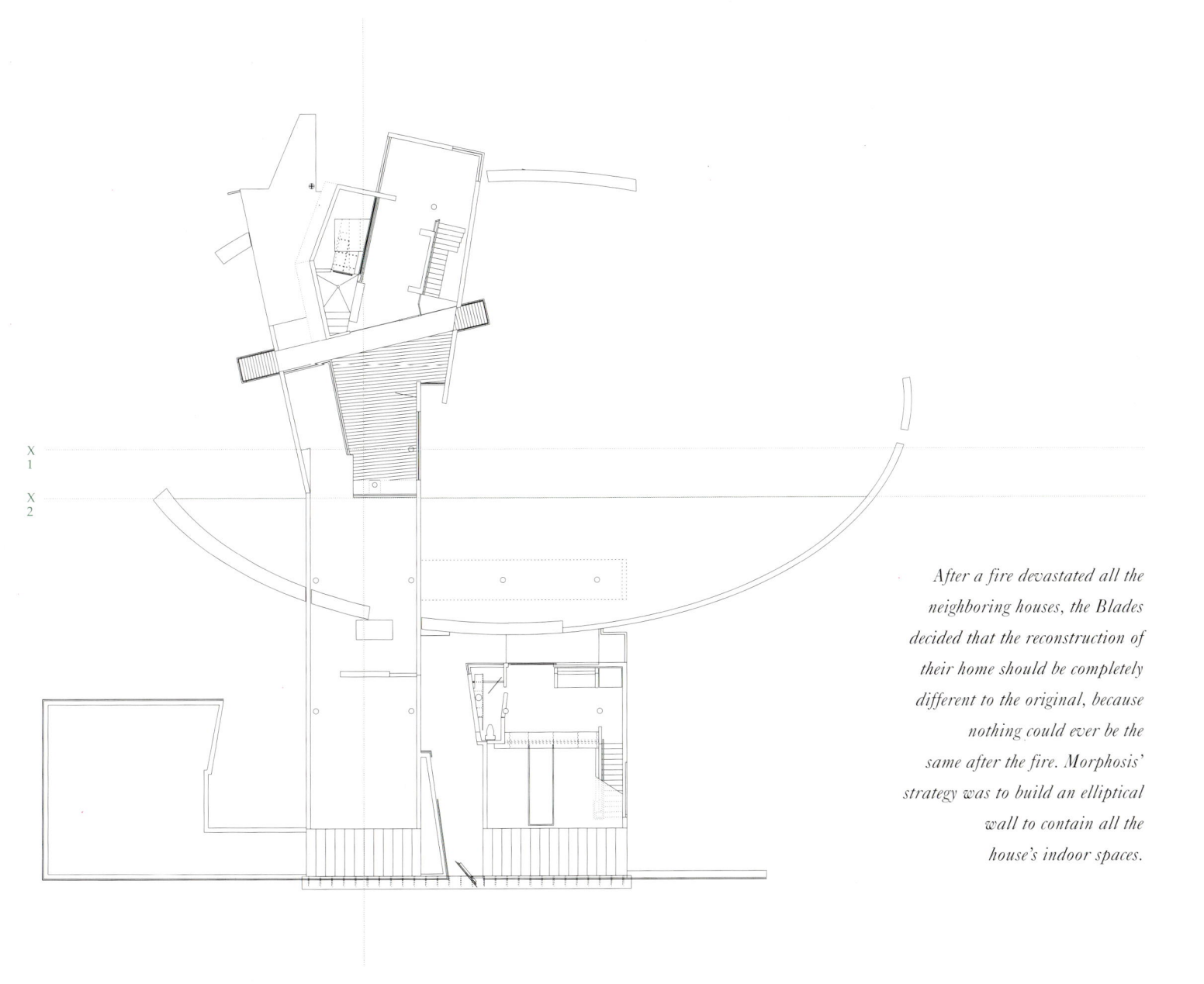

After a fire devastated all the neighboring houses, the Blades decided that the reconstruction of their home should be completely different to the original, because nothing could ever be the same after the fire. Morphosis' strategy was to build an elliptical wall to contain all the house's indoor spaces.

Hiroshi Nakao

1. *Coup de Sonde I-IV*
1990

2. *Black Maria*
1994

*House and Studio for an Ikebana Artist
1996*

Hiroshi Nakao is the youngest architect to appear in this book. He is certainly the most hermetic, too. Nakao cannot be pigeonholed into any single architectonic trend. Nor are his arguments what we usually find in architecture: program, structure, integration into the context.

All of his works have a conceptual and even ontological origin. Nakao's main theme of reflection is the empty space, a constant in Japanese culture where it has a completely different dimension to that of the West. In the city, in the house, in painting, the center is a void because it is a latent space; the place where things are to happen; where those on the watch, around its edges, direct their reflections and lucubration.

This is why Nakao's houses are black. They are waiting for the sun's rays to shine in through the windows and course through them. This is why both his sculptures and houses are made up of the mechanisms of stretching, rotation, compression, and extension of an empty but generating space at their center.

Hiroshi Nakao (Kobe, 1961) first studied architecture at the Kyoto Institute of Technology and then at the University of Tsukuba, graduating in 1989. In the same year, he set up his own studio and has been working freelance ever since.

His early works, Chairs for a Photographer (1989) and Coups de Sonde (1990) are a cross between furniture design and sculpture. He also took part in the exhibition of young artists in Zagreb in 1989.

His first work of architecture was a weekend home, which named Dark Box and Bird Cage, in 1991. In subsequent years, he has carried out a series of projects for single-family houses which he identifies with an initial: N (1992), S, A, and I (1993). In 1996 he built House with Studio for an Ikebana Artist in Tokorozawa.

In spite of his youth and a body of work which is, as yet, still small, his projects have received coverage in the leading Japanese journals GA, JA, SD and been exhibited both in his homeland and abroad; the prestigious AA in London devoted an exhibition to his work in 1996.

House and Studio for an Ikebana Artist

- **Location:** Torokawa, Japan.
- **Construction:** 1996.
- **Architect:** Hiroshi Nakao.
- **Associates:** Hiroko Serizawa.
- **Photographs:** Nacasa & Partners.

The outside walls are clad in steel which changes drastically from black to red as it rusts; then, it subtly and slowly changes back again. The house is submerged in the occurrence and recurrence of black. Like a laminar image sliding over the world, the black temporarily welcomes and silences all substance. All we have to do is sit down and wait. Wait for that which recovers the deepest memory and makes it speak: light.

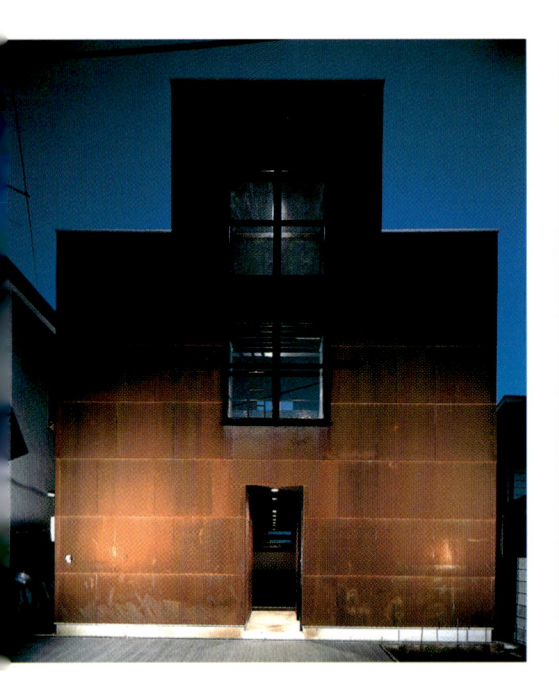

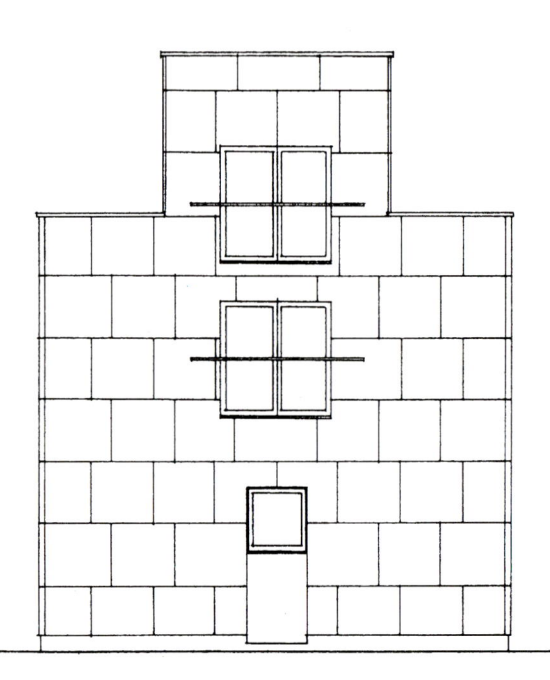

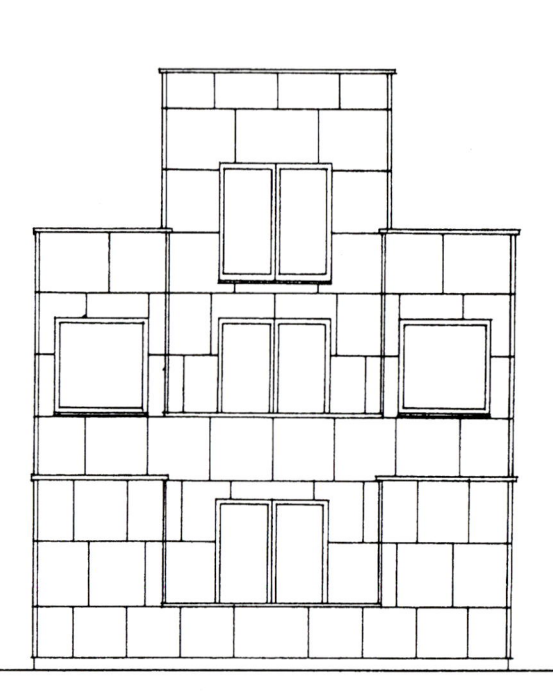

House and Studio for an Ikebana Artist

Eric Owen Moss

1. The Box
1993

2. Aronoff House
Project

3. Samitaur
1997

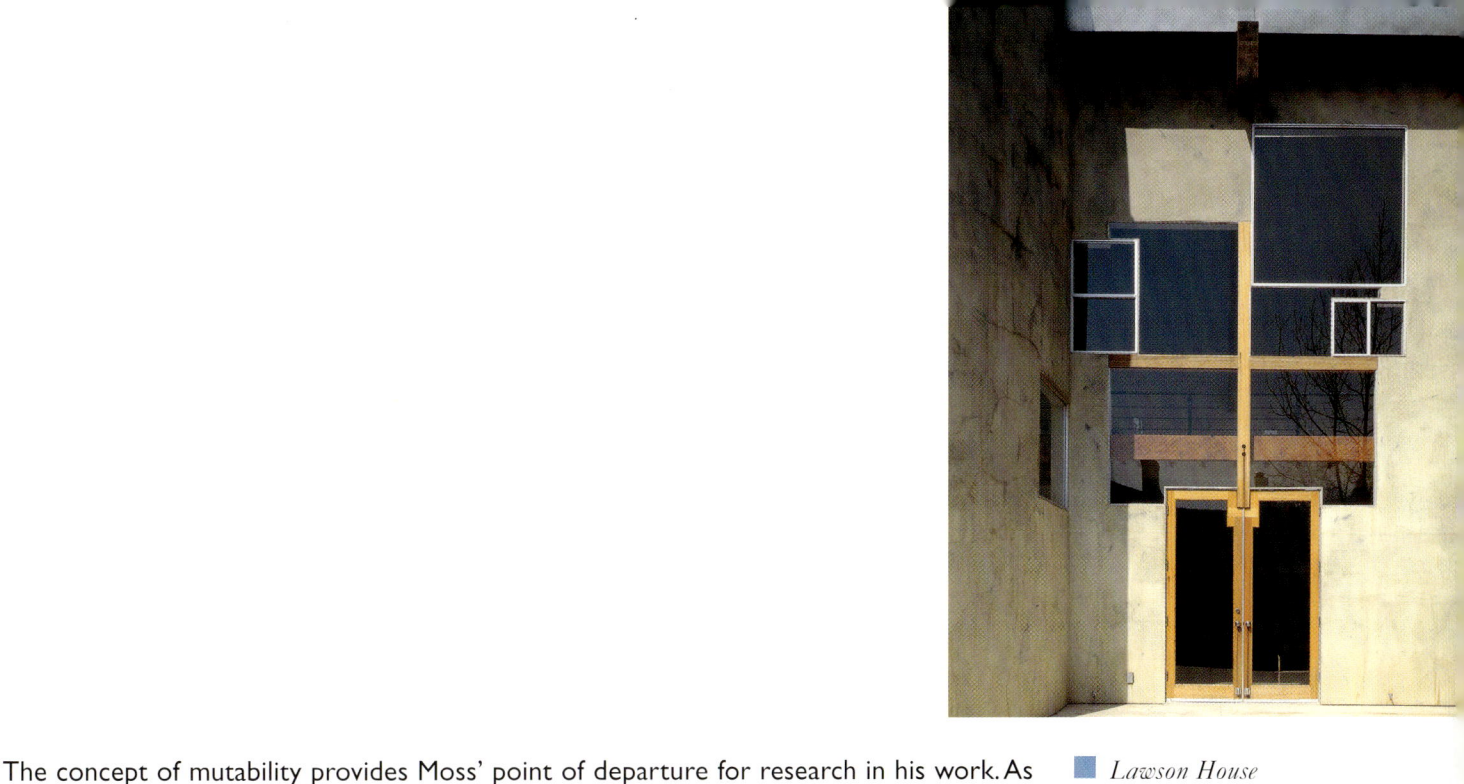

Lawson House 1992

The concept of mutability provides Moss' point of departure for research in his work. As part of the visual culture of deconstructivism and the tradition of Frank Gehry, his projects set forward a new approach by reformulating architectonic principles. The distortion of pure geometry is the starting point for his formal conceptions, marked by a manifest spatial ambiguity; one of the best examples of this is Lawson/Westen House (1988-1993), where the volume of the house stands out as the product of multiple geometric hybridations, which can also be seen in the planimetric studies. This formal complexity produces interesting results in indoor spaces, with unexpected entrances of light and perspectives, both highly dynamic artifices. The structural solutions of his buildings tend to be particularly complex, characterized by a high level of experimentation with materials. In some cases, his structural manipulations are taken to extremes: here we are thinking of Paramount Laundry, with its disproportionate down pipe-column, twisting capriciously at the corner to produce the visual instability of the roof.

Eric Owen Moss (1943) studied at the University of Los Angeles, graduating in 1965. In 1975, he set up Eric Owen Moss Architects. One of his first known projects was the restructuring of two old buildings—Lindable Tower and Paramount Laundry (California, 1987-1989)—which are visually connected by two porticoes with the characteristic down pipe-column. In 1988-1993 he designed Lawson/Westen House in California, an exploration of geometric hybrids. Between 1989-1995, he worked on his famous Samitaur high-rise building (Los Angeles, 1989-1995) with the corner that concentrates a series of geometric studies. Among his unbuilt projects are the entry for the competition for the Nara Convention Center (Japan, 1992), the promenade in Ibiza (1992), and Plaza Vieja in Havana (Cuba, 1994).

Lawson House

- **Location:** Brentwood, California, USA.
- **Construction:** 1992.
- **Architect:** Eric Owen Moss.
- **Associates:** Jay Vanos (associate architect), Gary David (structure), Grey Tchamitchian (installations), Saul Goldin (lighting), Roll Wilhite (landscape), John Blackley (contractor).
- **Photographs:** Tom Bonner.

The formal language, applied to both the interiors and the facades, obeys a series of very specific ideas as to domestic programs, with some mold-breaking results that still manage to reflect attention to detail and overall design, in what is a conceptual dissection of the home at all levels. Eric Owen Moss does not limit himself to engineering a harmonious organization of conventional spaces: he sees architecture as a way of exploring all the potential that any space has to offer.

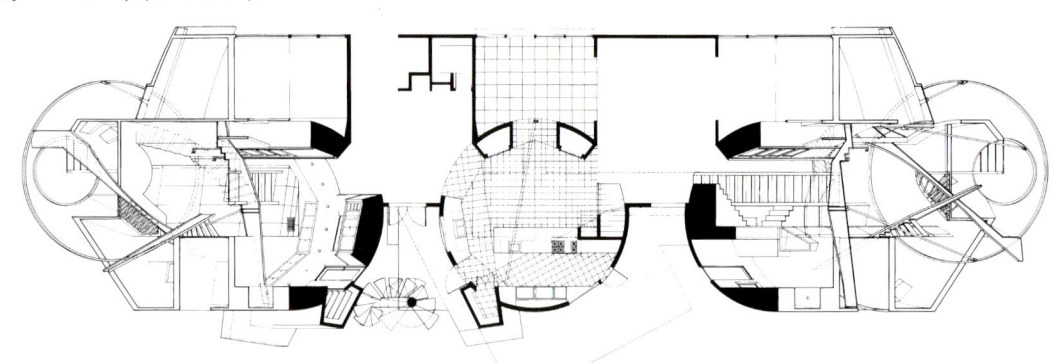

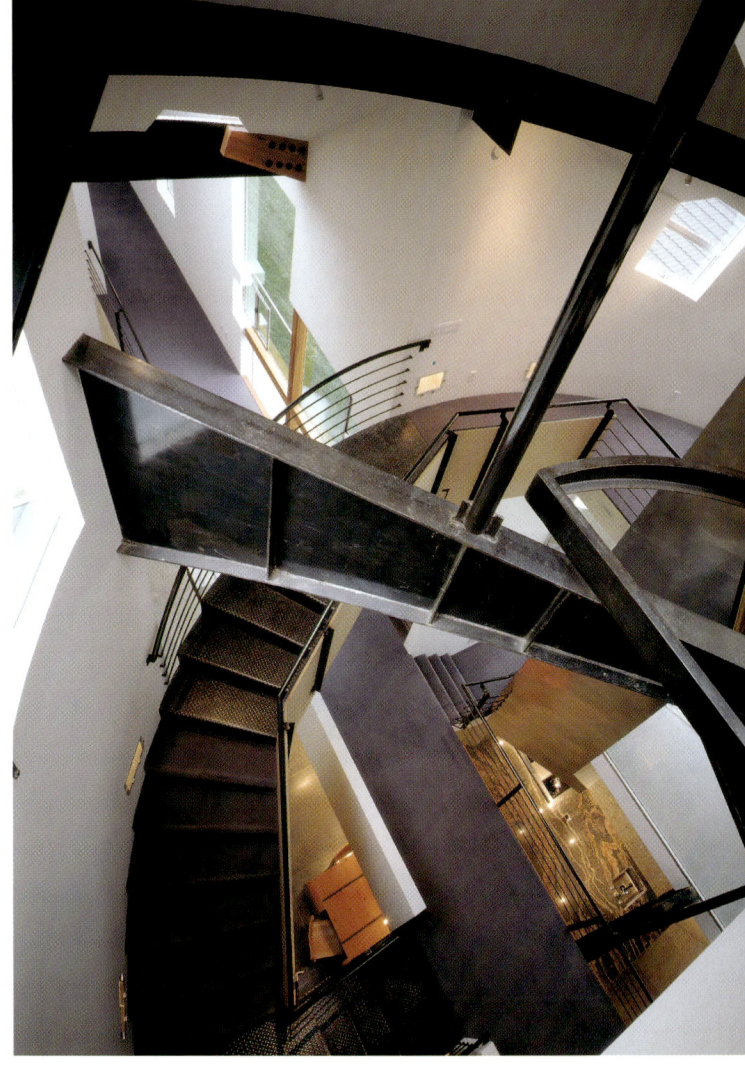

Eric Owen Moss

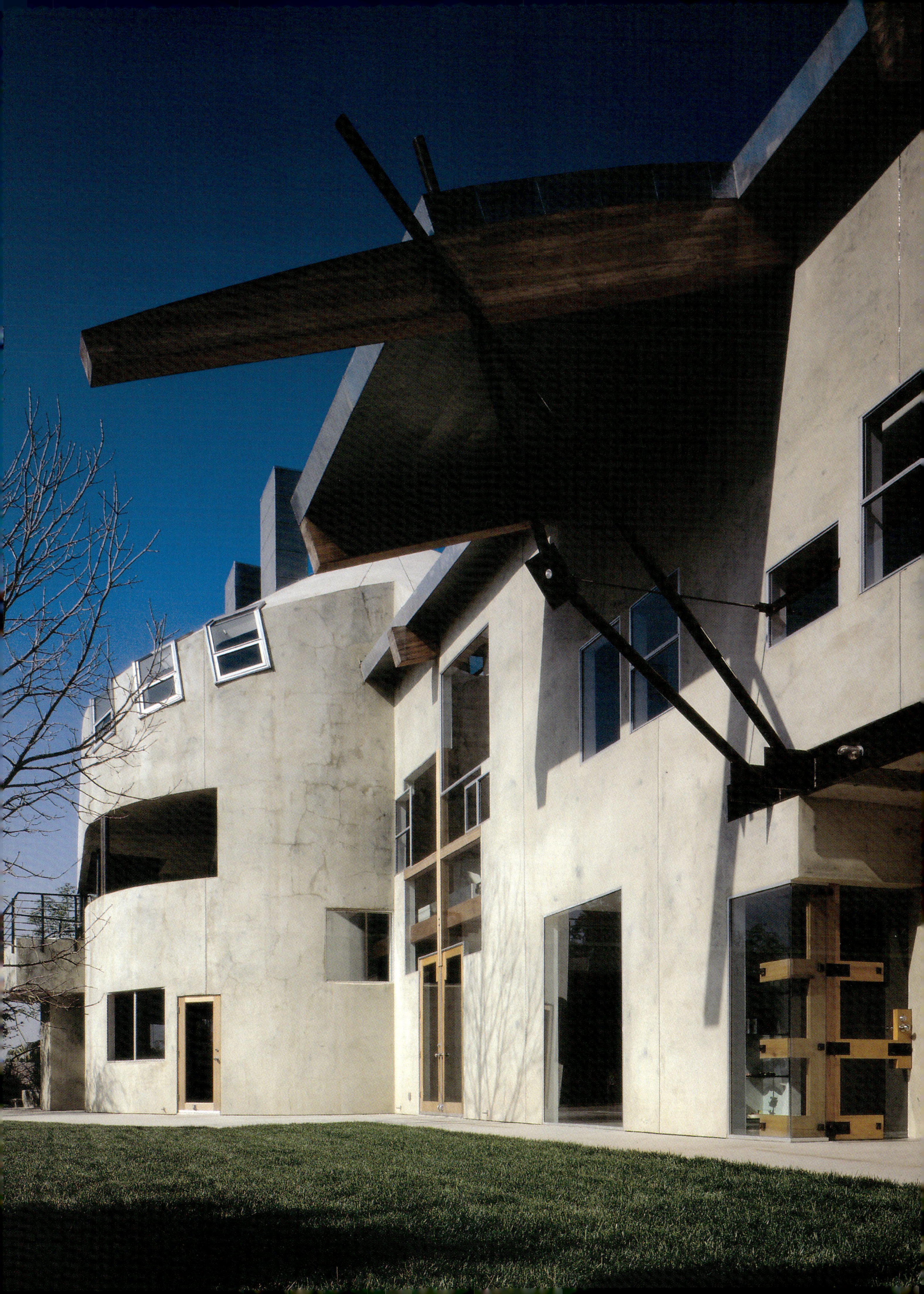

Nikken Sekkei

1. Fukuoka Tower
1989

2. Solid Square
1994

3. Japanese Long-term Credit Bank
1994

Osaka World Trade Center 1995

If by architecture studio we understand a freelance professional assisted by a dozen people, then Nikken Sekkei is the very opposite. This firm currently involves almost two thousand workers and has constructed buildings in forty countries. It is one of the world's largest architecture firms (S.O.M., Gensler, Kajima Design, Hellmuth, Obata & Kassabaum, etc.), which work on completely different lines than the small offices. Their staffs include hundreds of architects, and their invoicing is astronomical.

Nikken Sekkei is the longest established of these firms. What is more, unlike in the cases of Gensler or HOK, there is no visible head: it is an absolutely collective organization. It is run on the Japanese kaisha system, the company as an extended family in which all the employees work for their whole professional lives and, therefore, form a close-knit group in which there is no marked hierarchy.

The origins of Nikken Sekkei go back to the Meiji period (1868-1912), when it was set up as the architecture department of the Zaibatsu Sumitomo, in 1900. During the early decades, it produced an eclectic architecture which was Western in appearance. Under the direction of Eikichi Hasebe and Kenzo Takekoshi, the firm became independent. After the war, Nikken Sekkei started to grow at the same rate as the country itself. It stands out for its capacity for technological research and incorporation of new materials. Some of its computer design and structure calculation programs, such as Building, have become a reference for the entire Japanese construction industry.

Outstanding among its works are Tokyo Tower (1958)—a version of the Eiffel Tower—Kobe Tower (1964), the Hanshin motorway building in Osaka (1970), Nakano Sun Plaza in Tokyo (1973), Tokyo International Airport (1973), NS building in Shinjuku (1982), the new Sumitomo Corporation City (1984), and Tokyo Dome (1988), among hundreds of other buildings.

Osaka World Trade Center

- Location: Osaka, Japan.
- Construction: 1995.
- Architect: Nikken Sekkei.
- Photographs: Kouji Okamoto.

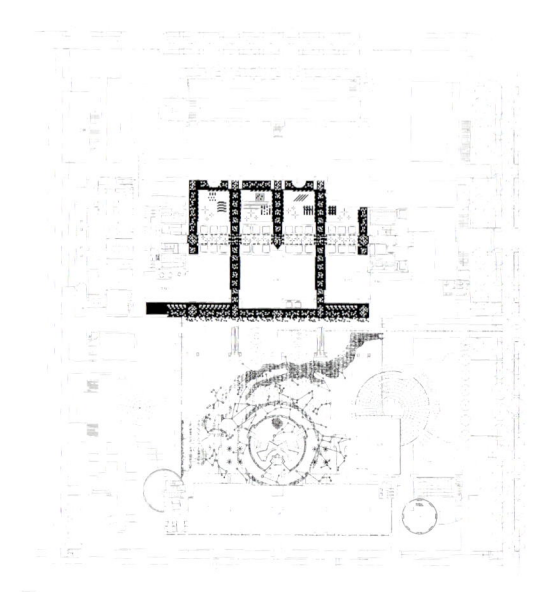

Technoport Osaka is a new extended urban center in Osaka Bay which is still under construction and is to cover almost 2,000 square yards of land distributed on the three artificial islands of Maishima, Yumeshima, and Sakishima. The World Trade Center Osaka (WTCO) is the most emblematic symbol of the district of Nanko, on the island of Sakishima. Standing over 280 yards high, it has 55 floors and a total surface area of some 18,000 square yards, which makes it the highest building in the west of Japan; it has rapidly become not just a symbol of the Cosmo Square coastline where it is situated, but also a visual reference for the entire bay and the Kansai region.

Jean Nouvel

1. Nemausus
1987

2. Institute of the Arab World
1987

3. Lyons Opera House
1993

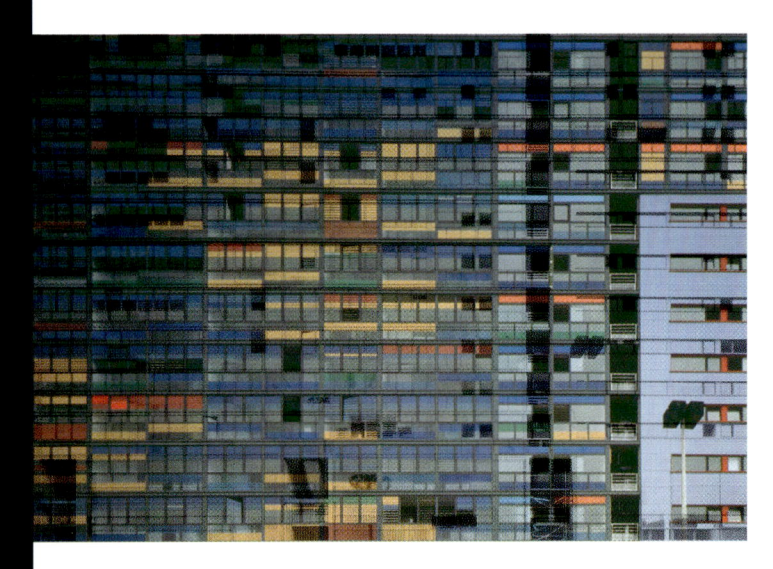

4. Triangle des Gares, Euralille
1994

5. Cartier Foundation
1994

*Galleries Lafayette
1996*

"Architecture is the introduction of the values of culture and civilization into the built environment." This statement by Jean Nouvel indicates his interest in works intended to excite emotions and sensations using the new symbolic codes promoted by today's urban and technological society. For Jean Nouvel, architecture has to crystallize the spirit of its time and lead to the spatial consolidation of a culture and an imaginary domain. In his case, the symbolic world to be captured is modernity. To this end, he takes "all the potential of the time" as his tools. His architecture feeds on the influences of the cinema, advertising, graphic art, and virtuality, as well as on the study of technological possibilities and the use of new materials; and he sets his sights very firmly on glass. Glass, seen not simply as a transparent material, but also as one which reflects, refracts, and manipulates light, allowing him to make an in-depth study of the theme of evanescence in the project and the imprecision of limits—of unreality, in short.

Jean Nouvel (Fumel, 1945) studied and started his working life at the time of May '68 in France. Nouvel played a fairly committed part in this movement, due to his professional relationship with one of its theoreticians, Paul Virilio, who later gave up architecture to devote himself to philosophy. Nouvel was one of the founders of the Mars 1967 movement, which adopted a very critical position on the prevailing bureaucracy and legal anachronisms in architecture.

In the early eighties, he won several competitions such as the one for the Institute of the Arab World in Paris and the social housing competition the French Government regularly organized at that time, for architects under the age of forty (later to become EUROPAN), and which led him to build the famous Nemausus blocks in Nîmes, along with Jean-Marc Ibos and Myrto Vitart.

After these projects, his international prestige grew and, in the nineties, he was responsible for large-scale projects such as Tours Congress Center, the Euralille Shopping Center, Lyons Opera House, and the Cartier Foundation in Paris, a company for which he has worked on several commissions.

Galleries Lafayette

- **Location:** Friedrichstad Passagen Block 207, Berlin, Germany.
- **Construction:** 1996.
- **Architect:** Jean Nouvel.
- **Associates:** Barbara Salin, Laurence Daude, Judith Simon, Vivienne Morteau.
- **Cost:** 211,000,000 DMarks.
- **Photographs:** Philippe Ruault.

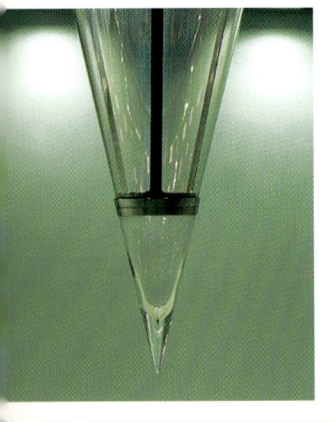

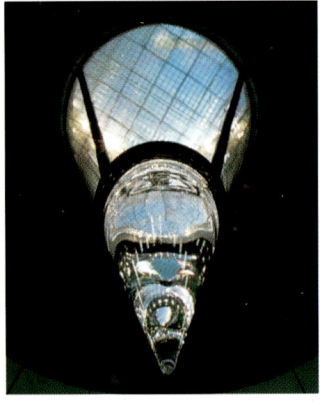

Nouvel designed a volume which is glazed on all sides (including the roof), to allow the interactive play of the daylight outside, the light shining in, and the artificial light generated by the building itself; the overall effect of the reflections creates an atmosphere which is both spectacular—responding to the characteristics of the activities going on within—and clearly functional—it does not interfere with the user-spectator's ability to find their way around.

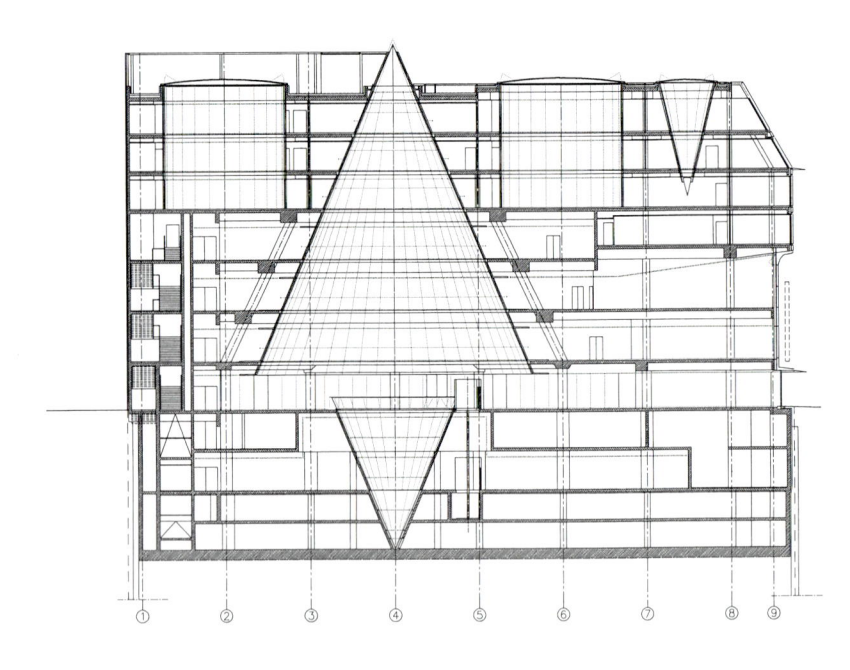

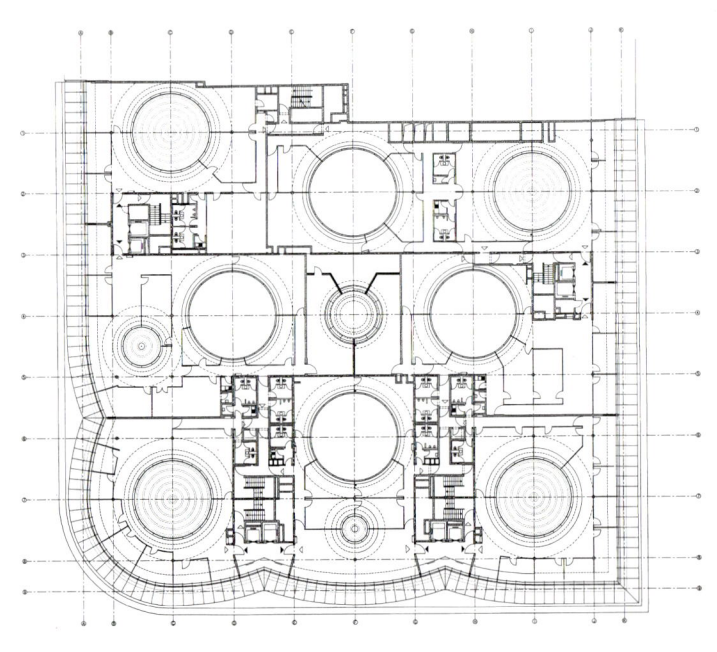

142 *Jean Nouvel*

Galleries Lafayette 143

César Pelli

1. Petronas Twin Towers
1997

2. NTT Headquarters
1995

3. World Financial Center
1988

Sea Hawk Hotel
1992

Pelli's professional career has basically unfolded amidst skyscrapers, contributing to a change in the skylines of various American cities. Pelli defines himself as a pragmatic architect, because he has frequently taken on large-scale projects, sometimes with limited budgets; this means that his proposals follow the indications of the project without bringing preconceived ideas to them. So each new response is potentially without precedent in his body of work, although there are some recurrent themes: the use of glass, for instance, to produce ambiguities and distortions on the outside, as opposed to clarity and order on the inside. One of his most interesting studies looks at the spatial relationships in communications laid out in the form of a backbone, which he practices both in his high-rise buildings and smaller-scale projects, where each space interconnects with another further down the hierarchy. On this theme, he developed one particularly interesting project: Long Gallery House (1980) where a great corridor-gallery links up the various volumes; this study led to the construction of Maryland House (1985-1989).

César Pelli (1926) graduated from the National University of Tucuman in Argentina. In 1952, he moved to the United States, where he studied at the University of Illinois. He worked in the studio of Eero Saarinen between 1954 and 1964. At Gruen Associates he designed various buildings, such as the Pacific Design Center in Los Angeles (California, 1975) and the United States embassy in Tokyo (Japan, 1972-1975). In 1977, he was appointed head of studies at the University of Yale and moved to New Haven (Connecticut) where he set up Pelli and Associates. He was responsible for the tower annex to the Museum of Modern Art in New York (1977-1984) and the competition entry for the World Financial Center (New York, 1981-1987). His work has gone on to extend beyond North American borders: in London he designed Canary Wharf Tower (1986-1991), and he has won competitions such as the passenger terminal at Kansai Airport (1988). Recently, he designed the Petronas Twin Towers in Kuala Lumpa (Malaysia, 1991-1997), the world's highest towers; also during that time, he designed the 30-floor tower block for the NTT headquarters (Tokyo, Japan, 1995) and Sea Hawke Hotel & Resort in Fukuoka (Japan, 1995).

Sea Hawk Hotel

Sea Hawk Hotel

- Location: Fukuoka, Japan.
- Construction: 1995.
- Architect: César Pelli.
- Photographs: Taizo Kurukawa, Osamu Murai, César Pelli, Yukio Yoshimura.

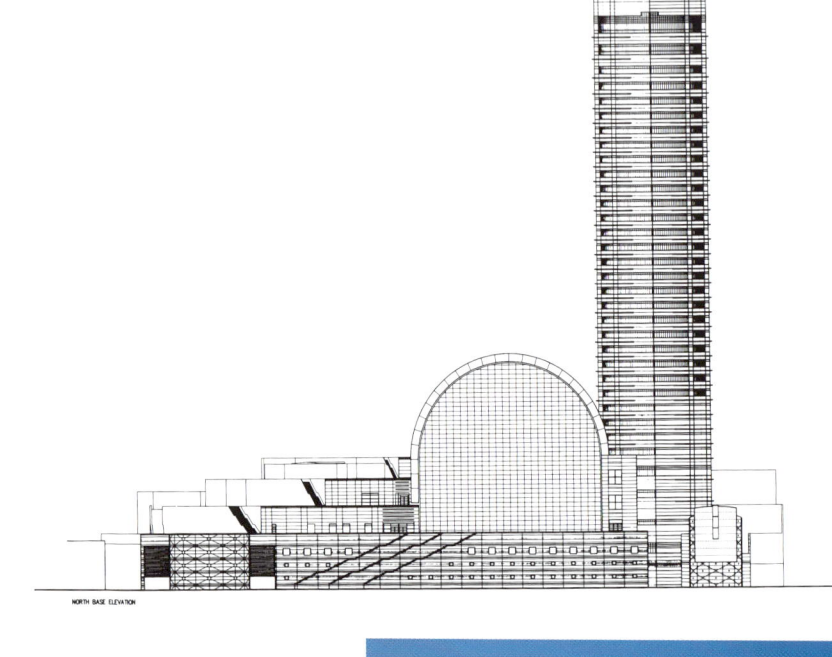

Pelli's projects all share a distinctive feature: a lack of preconceived ideas. Each project is designed according to place, climate, culture that is, its individual context. The volumes of his architectonic complexes are strong-lined and well defined. The materials are used in all their expressiveness and color, bursting forth into urban space with all the force of their character and personality.
The design of this seashore hotel, visible from the city and looming like a lighthouse, creates a composition of sculptural forms in the bay. The curves of the roof and walls relate to the elementsówater and wind. The walls of the hotel have a ceramic tile finish which forms a rich texture of different colors and designs.
Unlike in Western hotels, the complementary functions in Japan make up the living center of the hotel: halls for wedding banquets, luxury restaurants, bars, meeting rooms, and so on.

César Pelli

Sea Hawk Hotel

Dominique Perrault

1. Technical Book Center
   1995

2. Industrielle Hotel
   1990

The National Library of France 1994

While Perrault's work features a wide variety of textures, materials and colors, what characterizes his buildings is the austerity their external volumes are treated with; they become monumental complexes based on simplicity, seeking a degree of neutrality in their relationship with the context. The use of glass in his projects produces transparencies and reflections which tend, during daylight hours, to dissolve the volumes into the context, while enticing us to see them as clearly defined boxes of light at night. In more recent projects such as the Technical Book Center in Mame-la-Vallée, new materials are introduced into the facade, though its pure geometry is preserved. Even when using opaque elements, Perrault manages to maintain a feeling of transparency in his buildings. The spatial treatment given to their insides tends to evoke historical associations in the spectator, whether in the use of materials or the spatial characteristics, as in the French National Library in Paris.

Dominique Perrault (1953) started to work independently in 1981. When he won the competition for the French National Library in 1989, he had already designed buildings in which we could surmise the leitmotifs of his work: transparency, reflections, glass skins, etc. One particular example is the cubic volume of the Jean-Baptiste Berlier industrial building or the sewage treatment plant in Ivry-sur-Seine (1987-1993). Since designing his controversial National Library, Perrault has acquired international fame. This project is one of the great interventions promoted by Mitterrand in Paris and in it the architect sets out four volumes which become book towers, giving rise to a large empty space between them. Also in 1989 he won the competition for the Mayenne Department Archives (Laval, France), where he had to extend a nineteenth century building to twice its original surface area. The proposal consisted of a blind, very sober-lined volume which he placed back-to-back with the old building, with all due respect for its proportions. Later on, his treatment of facades gradually extended to include different materials, but he has never turned his back on the rigorous geometry which distinguishes the Technical Book Center in Mame-la-Vallée (1995), where aluminum becomes the main element in the facade.

The National Library of France

- Location: Paris, France.
- Construction: 1994.
- Architect: Dominique Perrault.
- Photographs: Georges Fessy.

Everyone who enters this controversial building is fascinated by its simplicity, its lack of ostentation, and by a modernity that shuns the concept of a single viewpoint or perspective to stress the sensorial: touch (the change from asphalt to wood), smell (rain, woods), sound (wind, muffled noises), and sight (exceptional distances of over 300m. separate the towers). The recurring use of materials is marked by a singular sensibility, devoid of any desire for ornamentation. Each part of the building is characterized by the specific use of materials: towers enveloped in glass with a second skin of wood; the esplanade and paths, also in wood; the four buildings beneath the towers, woven in steel framework; the red-carpeted reading rooms; wooden furniture and roofs of great meshes of stainless steel suspended from the wall across the garden in this case the contrast of materials is based on steel rather than on glass.

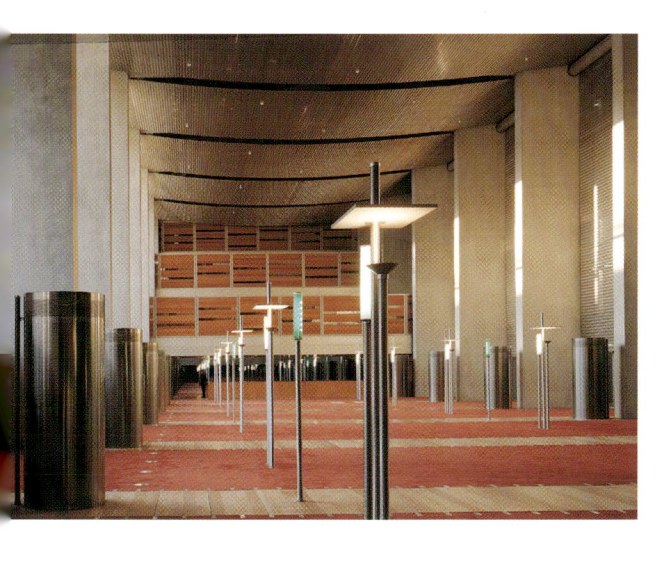

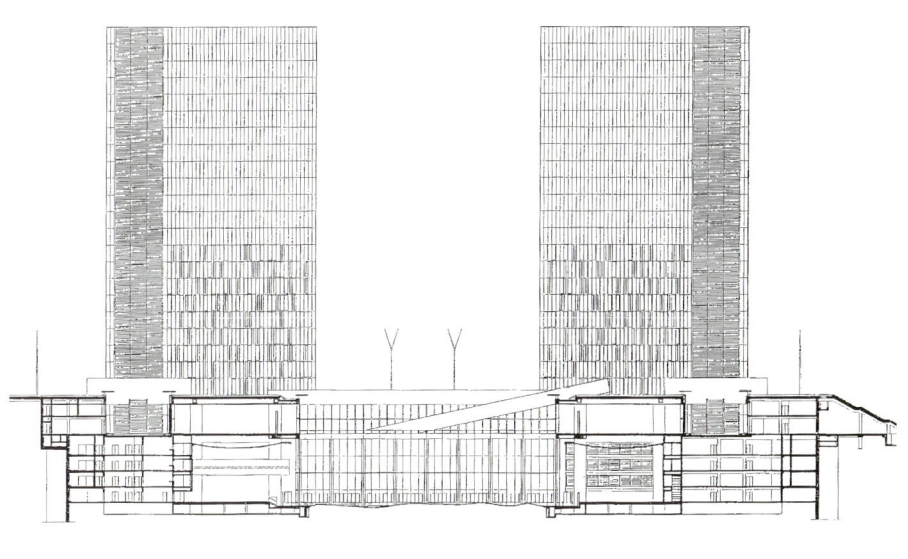

The National Library of France 151

Renzo Piano

1. The De Menil Collection
1986

2. Bari Stadium
1989

3. Kansai Airport
1995

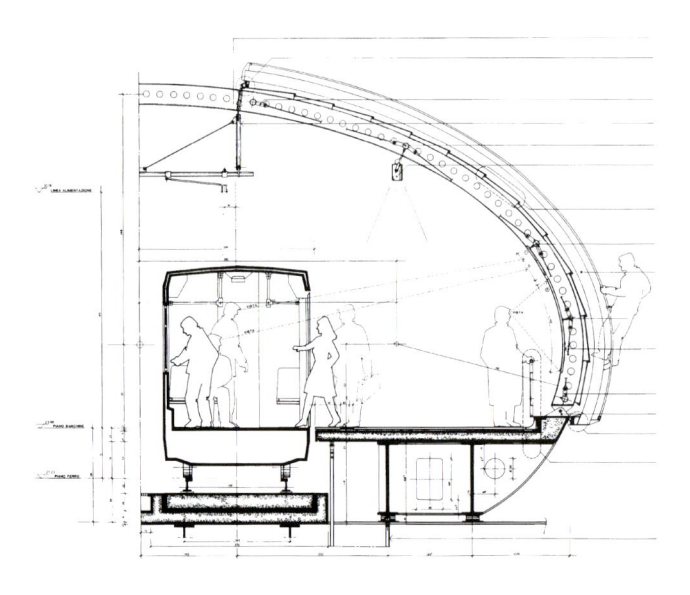

4. A Stretch of the Genoa Subway
1990

*The Cy Twombly Annex
1995*

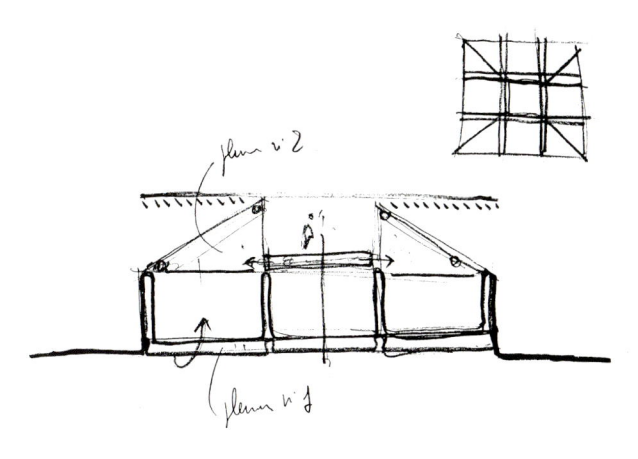

Renzo Piano has frequently been heard to confess that his aim is to seek out the human side of technology, to reclaim for major infrastructures the spirit of the minor craftsman who carefully works the details of a precious object.

In fact, since the Centre Pompidou (his acclaimed first building, in collaboration with the British architect Richard Rogers), Piano has always applied technology to reinforce light, context, and the possibility of integration into nature. While the Pompidou is industrial in appearance, the rest of Piano's work is motivated by ecological concerns technology has ceased to be the means and the end, and is now just a means. This approach has led him to direct certain remodeling projects and combine his studio's activity with that of the Unesco laboratory in Vessina.

The sections are particularly interesting in Piano's works; in this architectonic projection his buildings mature; also, as a result of the particular emphasis he places on bringing daylight into his buildings, almost all of his projects are based around the construction of the roof.

Renzo Piano (Genoa, 1937) studied architecture at the Polytechnic in Milan. Since winning the competition to design the Centre Pompidou in Paris (1971) along with Rogers, Piano has become a prominent figure on the international architecture scene, with more works constructed outside Italy than in his own country.

Piano brings a similar approach to both the small and the large scale. He has directed projects of very varying sizes: small buildings like the traveling IBM Pavilion, the Cy Twombly Annex, and the Brancusi Museum opposite the Pompidou; and great megastructures like Kansai's International Airport Terminal built on a man-made island in the Bay of Tokyo, Bari Stadium, and the remodeling of Berlin's Potsdamer Platz where work is scheduled to be completed in 2002.

The Cy Twombly Annex

- **Location:** Houston, Texas, USA.
- **Construction:** 1992.
- **Architect:** Renzo Piano.
- **Associates:** S. Ishida, M. Carroll, M. Palmore.
- **Photographs:** Hichey + Robertson.

Five years after the main building was opened, Dominique de Menil commissioned Renzo Piano to design a small annex to the museum, covering 1,000 square yards, to be devoted to the work of the American artist Cy Twombly. In appearance, this annex differs from the main building, at the express desire of both owner and architect, yet they share the same concern: lighting. In association with Ove Arup, lighting studies were carried out at the Architecture and Urban Design Faculty in Michigan. A model of the building was placed on a large spherical mirror, and a complex system of computer-produced spotlights was projected onto it; the movement and brightness of the Houston sun was thereby reproduced with a view to studying its effects on the inside of the building.

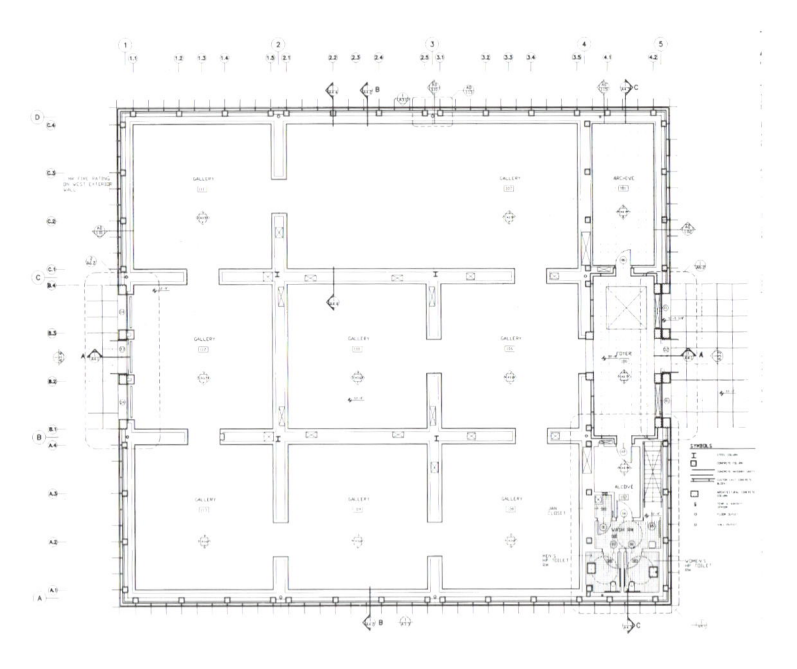

Renzo Piano

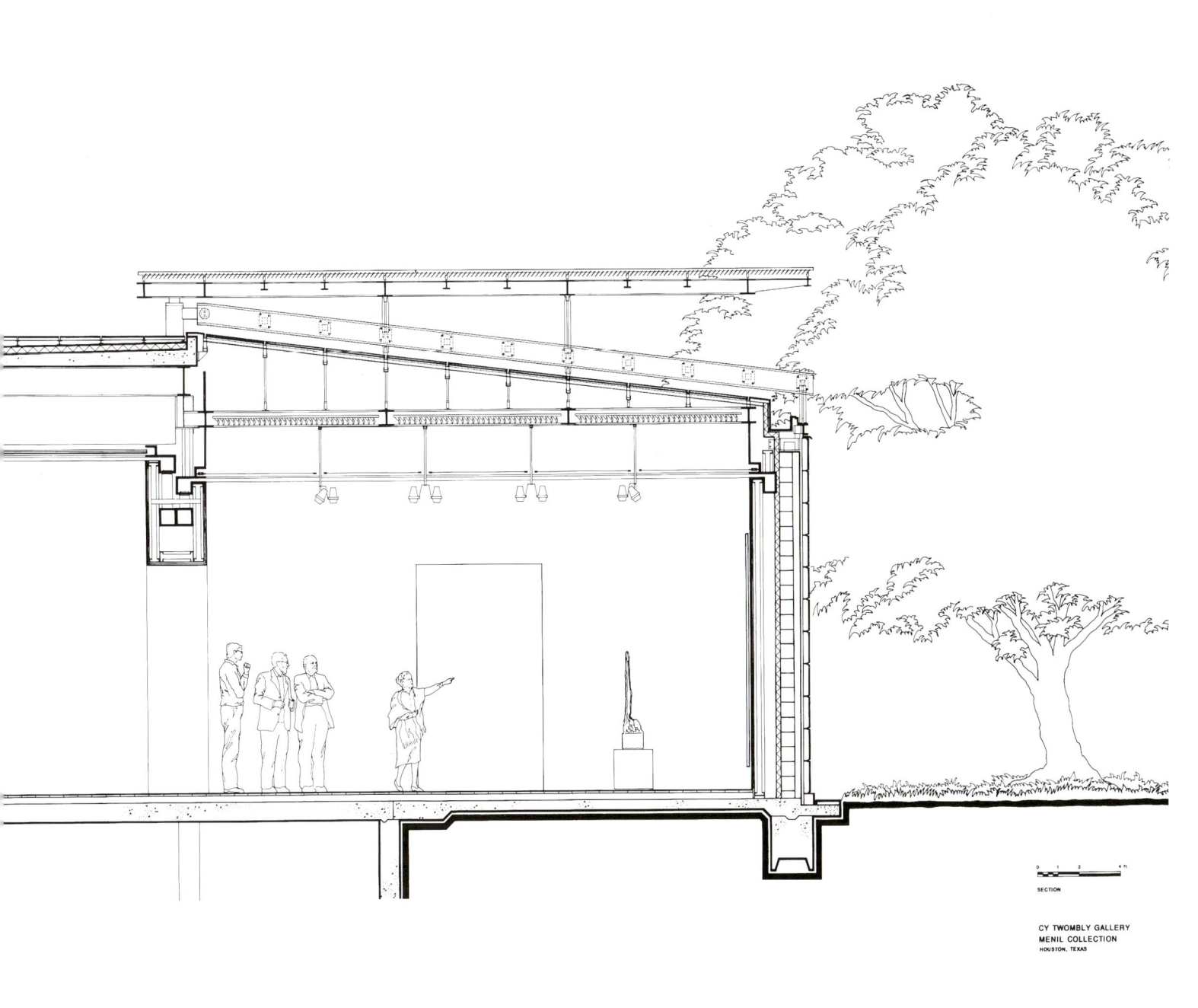

CY TWOMBLY GALLERY
MENIL COLLECTION
HOUSTON, TEXAS

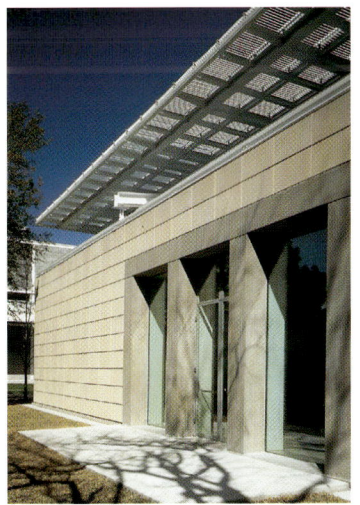

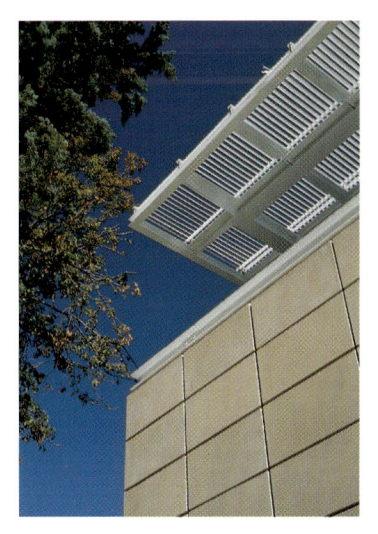

The Cy Twombly Annex   155

Gabriel Poole

1. House at Noosa Heads
1990

2. House at Lake Weyba
1991

*Poole Residence
1996*

In the mid-eighties, Gabriel Poole developed a prototype of a house with a tent-like metal skeleton, which could be varied in all kinds of ways according to the program, the location, and the particular taste of the client in question. Rather than an exception to his body of work, this proposal is the result of his particular way of looking at architecture.

Gabriel Poole remains true to the pioneering spirit. His homes look as though you could almost put them together yourself. For Poole, the form is not as important as the construction system and choice of materials. This Queenslander almost always works with light structures which are slightly raised above the site rather than completely settling on it. For the walls and roof he uses corrugated metal sheet to give his constructions an industrial or even temporary appearance. Gabriel Poole is quite at home with this rather unpurist language, and very attached to the architecture of the colonizers and the appearance of settlements in territories still unurbanized.

Gabriel Poole (Queensland, 1934) gave up his studies at the age of seventeen to spend the next five years as a sailor and foreman in the outback. He then started his architecture studies at the Queensland Institute of Technology, working with the professional studios of first Theo Thynne and then Robin Gibson. In 1967, he set up his own studio in Brisbane, to move later deeper into Queensland, to the towns of Mooloba, Noosa, and finally, Eumundi.

Since then, Gabriel Poole has devoted himself to the construction of houses in this touristic region of Australia. Among his projects, particular mention should be made of Tent-House (1985), the house at Noosa Head (1990), the house at Lake Weyba (1991), and his own house, also at Lake Weyba (1996).

Poole Residence

- **Location:** Noosa Heads, Australia.
- **Construction:** 1996.
- **Architect:** Gabriel Poole.
- **Associates:** Elisabeth Poole (design), Rod Bligh-Bligh Tanner (structure), Barry Hamlet (aluminum).
- **Photographs:** Peter Hyatt.

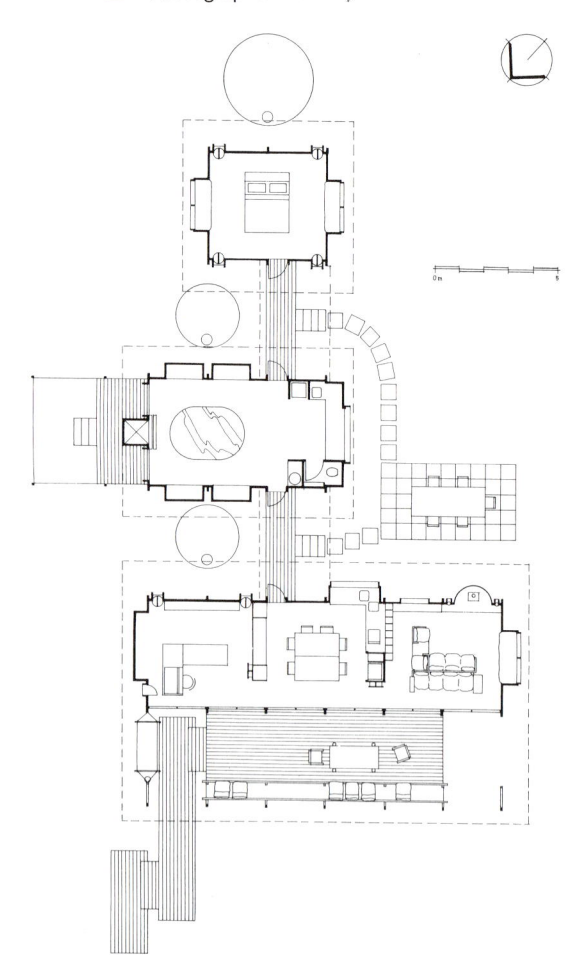

Poole organizes the space into three different pavilions, following the brief for a home. The entrance pavilion, at one end, contains the kitchen, dining room, and living room-cum-studio. The surface area covered can be doubled by opening up the vinyl and steel panels, to create a porch area. The outer limits of the inner space can be constantly changed by rearranging the moving partitions and extending the floor space beyond the lines marked by structure. In the second pavilion, we find the bathing area, including shower and wash basin. The color used for some of the surfaces (contrasting with the monochrome fiber-cement walls), the light, and the views of nature from indoors, are all conducive to relaxation and meditation before we go on to the third pavilion, where we find the master bedroom.

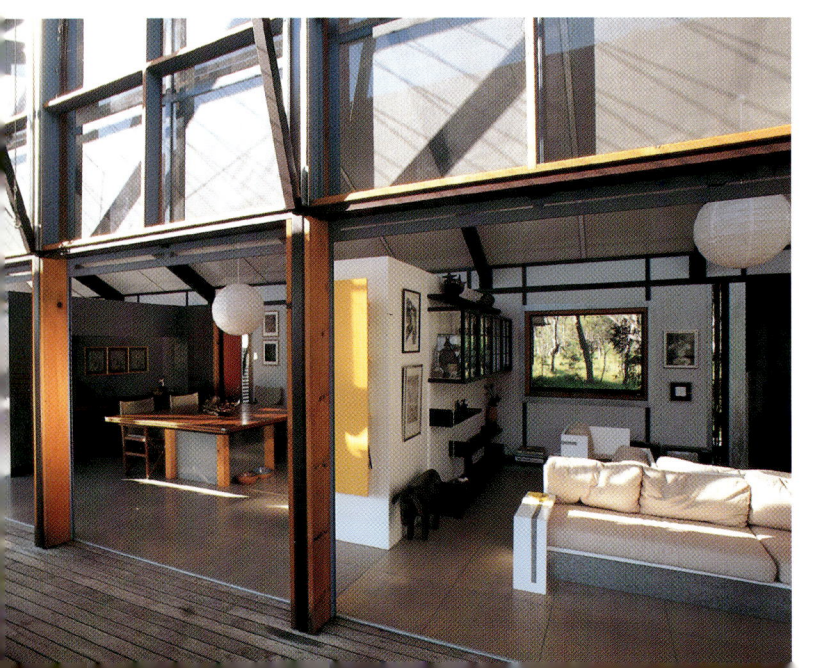

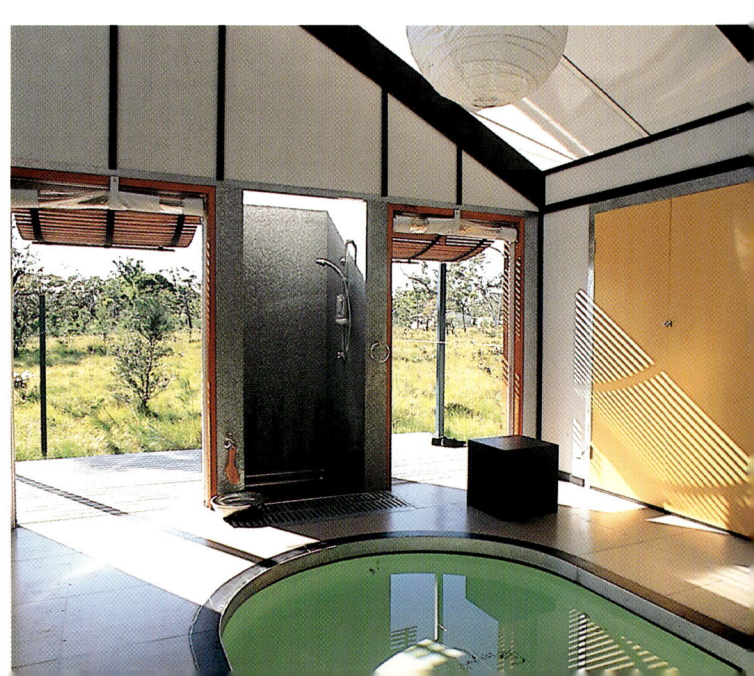

Poole Residence | 159

Antoine Predock

1. American Heritage Center
1987

2. House in Venice
1990

3. House in Paradise Valley
1989

Mesa Public Library 1994

We cannot help associating Predock's work with that of some of the masters of modern architecture: his work is the result of the "inspiration" of place and the variety of cultural influences in New Mexico, suggesting common ground with Frank Lloyd Wright. His architecture is the product of complex relationships, charging itself with a mystic aura, reminiscent of some of Kahn's representations. In fact, Predock's relationship to the latter was much more direct: among his early works, starting in the late sixties, we come across formal solutions similar to those of the master. He was quick to abandon this path, however, relegating any references to Kahn to simple one-off features inside the building, such as the stairway with overhead lighting in the Children's Museum in Las Vegas (1986-1990). His later work approaches the project as though it were a "choreographic event"; this, together with the change in scale of his commissions, has led him to design buildings with a variety of exterior volumes (almost all elemental) which become part of the desert landscape, or turn to theatrical effects like the sea which "comes into" the house in Venice (Los Angeles, 1988-1991).

Antoine Predock, based in Albuquerque (New Mexico), studied at the University of New Mexico and the University of Columbia, and graduated in 1962. Since 1967, he has had his own studio. His initial references to Kahn's aesthetics, which can be seen in the La Luz Community building in Albuquerque (New Mexico, 1967-1974), were left behind after the project for Fuller House in Scottsdale (Arizona, 1984-1987), although the Children's Museum in Las Vegas (1986-1990) still has a few features which are suggestive of the master. His relationship with place led him to investigate the field of cultural diversity; this research produced the American Heritage Center and the University of Wyoming Museum of Art in Laramie (1986-1993), where the two volumes of the project each represent a culture. He has designed projects for the Disney empire, such as the Hotel Santa Fe (France, 1988-1992), with its recourse to desert conventions. His most recent projects are the New York Museum and Art Gallery (1996) and his entry for the Copenhagen Archives competition (1997).

Mesa Public Library

- **Location:** Los Alamos, New Mexico, USA.
- **Construction:** 1994.
- **Architect:** Antoine Predock.
- **Associates:** Geoffrey Beebe (director and partner), Paul Gonzales, Breatt Oaks (project directors), Rebecca Ingram, George Newlands, Deborah Waldrip, Linda Christenson, John Brittingem, Cameron Erdmann, Geoff Adams, Mark Donahue (project team).
- **Photographs:** Timothy Hursley.

The layout and form of the indoor spaces are marked by a division in the program: the wedge houses the foyers, stairways, meeting rooms, and individual reading seats; and the large curved volume is a single space which holds the book shelves. The program called for a division between fiction and non-fiction, and between adults' and children's reading. Unlike other libraries, here the book storage surface is far larger than the reading space. Rather than having a main reading room, many of the individual tables are slipped in between the shelves and in front of the windows.

Mesa Public Library

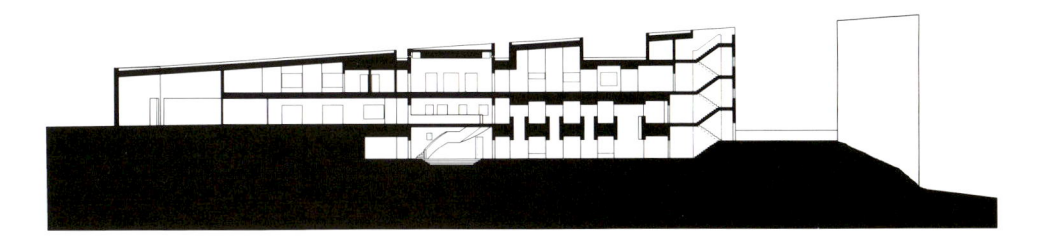

Kazuyo Sejima

1. *Pachinko Parlor II*
   1993

2. *Villa in the Woods*
   1994

*Pachinko Parlor III
1996*

It is very difficult to look at Kazuyo Sejima's work to date in isolation from that of Toyo Ito. In some cases, like in the House in the Woods in Tateshina (1994), the reference to a project by Ito, White U House (1976) is direct. In others, the connection takes the form of certain elements, like the roofs of PLATFORM I or the generous use of translucent glass in the Saishunkan Seiyaku women's dormitory.

Their bodies of work can, to some extent, be studied together. Ito and Sejima are, perhaps the two professionals who have done most to introduce the aesthetics of computing and virtual reality into architecture. While Ito's ultimate objective is to work with the ephemeral, Sejima aims to integrate signs into space.

The task that Sejima has set for herself is no superficial one. In a country like Japan (which Barthes christened the Empire of the Signs) and in an epoch like ours, where the vision of reality is filtered through screens and publications that always incorporate texts and signs, this is no mean feat.

Kazuyo Sejima (Ibaraki, 1956) studied architecture at the Women's University in Japan, graduating in 1981. She worked for six years in Toyo Ito's studio, before setting up Kazuyo Sejima & Associates in 1987.

In little over a decade, Sejima has become an international figure on the architecture scene. Even her early projects, PLATFORM I (1988), PLATFORM II (1990), and PLATFORM III (1990) received a great deal of projection and were awarded prizes. In the early nineties, she designed the Saishunkan Seiyaku women's dormitory (1991), received second prize in the top-level competition for the construction of La Maison de la Culture de Japon in Paris and had two consecutive one-woman exhibitions in Tokyo (Panasonic and MA galleries). In 1992, she was named Young Architect of the Year by the Japanese Institute of Architects. 1993 saw the completion of two Pachinko Parlor buildings.

Between 1994 and 1997 she designed several single-family houses: Villa in the Woods (1994), Y House (1994), S House (1997), and M House (1997). She is currently working on larger-scale projects, including several museums.

Pachinko Parlor III

- Location: Hitachiohta, Ibaraki, Japan.
- Construction: 1996.
- Architect: Kazuyo Sejima.
- Structure: Matsui Genko & O.R.S.
- Built surface area: 8000 sq. ft.
- Photographs: Nacasa & Partners Inc.

Pachinko is an extremely popular game in Japan, and one that combines chance with skill. The layout in rows of pachinko machines provided the inspiration for a volume in keeping with the activity going on inside: basically rectangular, and curving to follow the line of the freeway which it borders. The curvature of the facade and the use of light and materials provided a high enough profile to require just a humble sign to announce the name of the establishment, in which glossy black strips frame colored glass fragments. During the day, the black gloss smoothly returns reflections, while at night, the light inside the building sees these strips disappear to become a framework which outlines the facade.

Kazuyo Sejima

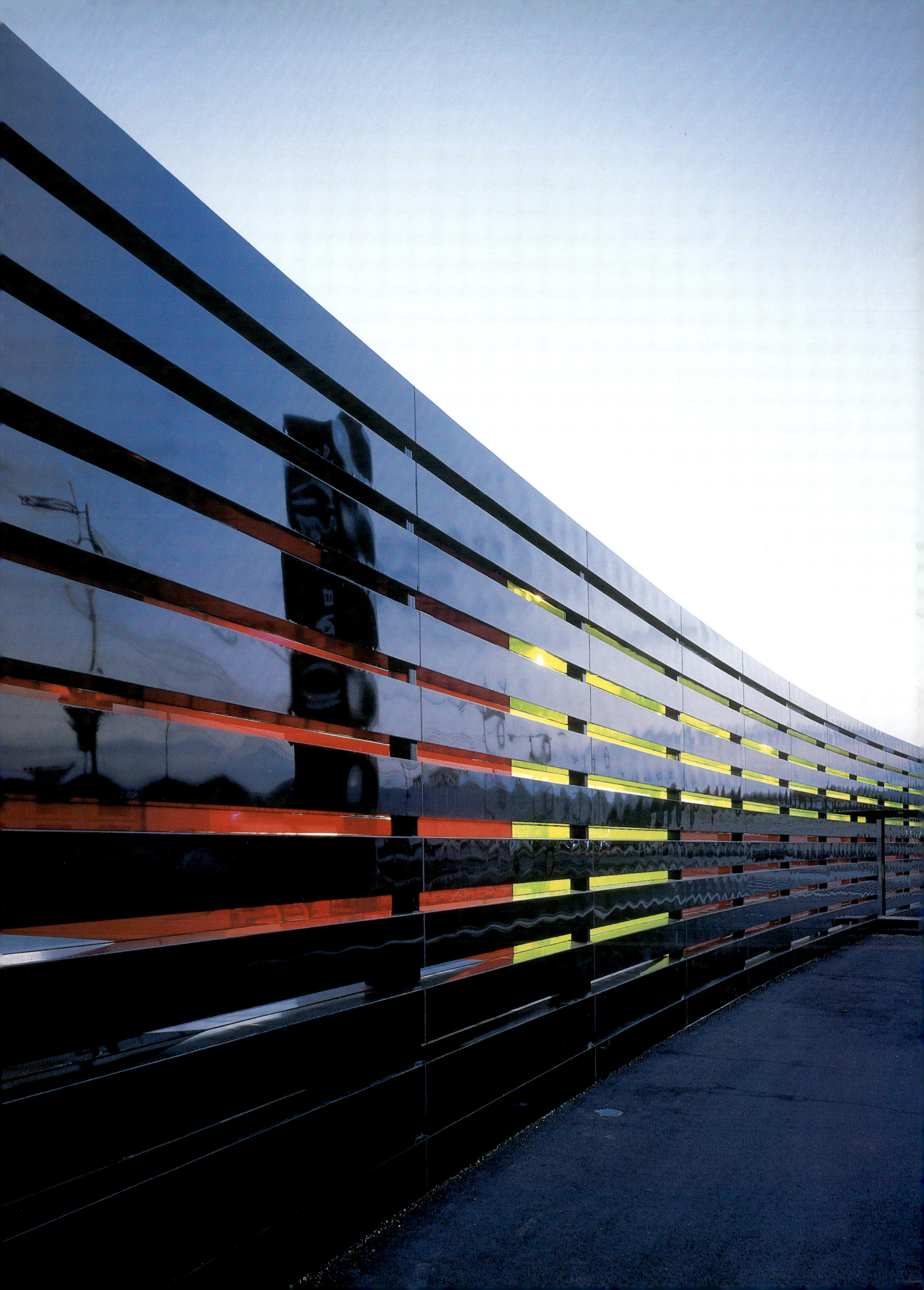

Naoyuki Shirakawa

1. Circle House
1996

2. Small House
1996

3. Toto Head Offices
1994

Cube House
1991

Shirakawa's architecture is based on geometrical principles and pure volumes which produce balanced projects. He frequently uses simple figures such as the cube or sphere, transforming them to reveal a degree of spatial complexity.

Many of his projects—particularly his family houses—are variations on a single spatial theme. This leads to a Cube House, a Cube House II, and a Cube House III, which convey the importance of geometry and pure forms in his architecture.

However, there is no uniformity of spaces in Shirakawa's buildings. His projects are based on the contrast between opposing situations and polarity: dark and light, full and empty, active and passive, closed and open.

The outer simplicity of his works is to some extent a reaction to the disorder of the context. In this sense, many of his buildings open out onto private inner courts where a degree of control is possible.

Naoyuki Shirakawa (Kitakyushu-city, 1951) studied architecture at the University of Kyoto, graduating in 1974. Then, until 1987, he worked in association with the studio of Ishimoto Architects & Associates in Tokyo, later setting up his own office with the name of Naoyuki Shirakawa Atelier.

Most of his work has been produced in the nineties, with projects such as the Village 24 housing complex in Tochigi (1990), the family homes Cube House (Tokyo, 1991), Cube House II (Fukuoka, 1992), Small House (Fukuoka, 1996), Circle House (Fukuoka, 1996), and Small House II (Kobe, 1998), in addition to the factory of the Toto Bathroom Fittings firm in Fukuoka (1994).

Although these projects are not significant in terms of size, almost all of his works have been awarded prizes.

Cube House

- **Location:** Tokyo, Japan.
- **Construction:** 1991.
- **Architect:** Naoyuki Shirakawa.
- **Associates:** Sayuri Ikenone, Yasuhi Shikano, Hiroshi Miyamae, Chie Kudo, Aya Watanabe, Rosula Blam.
- **Photographs:** Koji Kobayashi.

The house is built in the center of Tokyo, on a narrow plot of land covering 84 square yards. It is a cube which measures 6.5 x 6.5 x 6.5 yards. The facade is simple in composition, with abstract forms organized on a square base. It can be seen as a plane for experimentation with compositional elements which are simple in both form and material. The entire project is based on geometry, with each element produced by parameters and processes of geometrical origin.

Cube House **171**

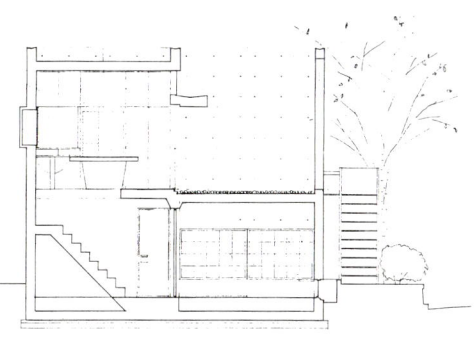

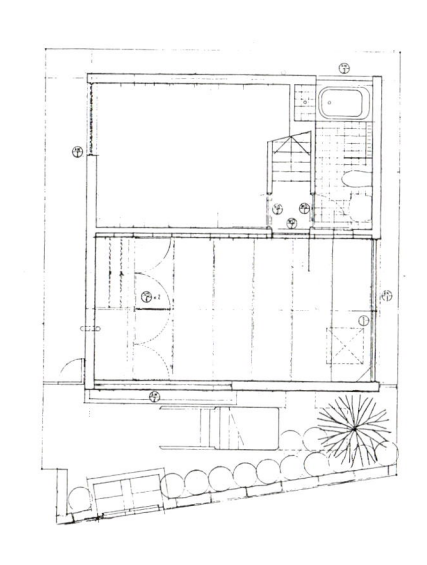

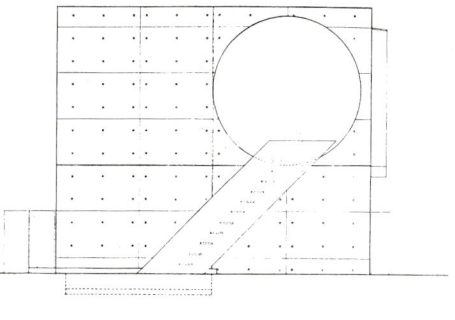

Álvaro Siza

1. School of Sciences of the Image
1994

2. Galician Center for Contemporary Art
1995

Santo Domingo de Bonaval Park 1994

People often try to see the architecture of Alvaro Siza as an isolated phenomenon in today's architectonic tradition. However his work is founded on many of the bases of rationalism; to some extent it follows the footsteps of Aalto, with a more thorough research of the "artistic" side of his work, and it also transforms sentient traces into modifications, all in the modern tradition.

The importance Siza concedes to place has been manifest throughout his career (which started in 1954). This is reflected in his planning method: he makes sketches on site or very close by, and in some cases uses that very drawing as the basis for the proposal here we are thinking of the swimming pool in Leça da Palmeira (1961-1966). However, this relationship with place is based on dialogue rather than mimesis; it responds to the conditioning factors of the urban site without compromising the architectural style. This means that his buildings are autonomous within the context, and are resolved by means of clear, simple volumetric study, subject to geometric manipulation in the form of twisting, intersection, fracture, and so on, to inject the whole with dynamism in terms of form and space.

Alvaro Siza (1933) studied at the School of Architecture of the University of Oporto. Between 1955 and 1958 he worked in the studio of Fernando Távora. He embarked on his professional career with the Boa Nova Restaurant (Leça da Palmeira, Portugal, 1958-1963). In this initial phase, his works combined modern typology with the vernacular tradition, as in the case of Beires House in Póvoa do Varzim, 1973. Nonetheless, he constantly returns to clear volumes, like the great white parallelepiped of Avelino Duarte House (Ovar, 1981-1985), which brings together all his earlier experience of housing typologies, although his major intervention in this area was the 1,200 homes built in Quinta da Malagueira (Évora, 1977). The most explicit example of "manipulation" of place is the swimming pool in Leça da Palmeira (1961-1966), where the curves and differences in level of the place produce the project. Since the eighties, he has been commissioned to carry out a wide variety of projects, ranging from the Oporto School of Architecture (1985-1993) and the Santiago de Compostela Museum of Contemporary Art (1988-1993) to the School of Education in Setúbal (1986-1992).

Santo Domingo de Bonaval Park

- **Location:** Rúa da Caramoniña, Santiago de Compostela, Spain.
- **Construction:** 1994.
- **Client:** Consortium of the City of Santiago de Compostela.
- **Arquitecto:** Alvaro Siza.
- **Associates:** Alessandro D'Amico, Xorxe Nuno and Carlos Muro.
- **Photographs:** Tino Martínez.

The Park de Bonaval, with a surface area of 35,000 m², occupies the grounds of the twelfth-century convent, which is divided into three clearly differentiated areas: a terraced vegetable garden at the lowest part near the new museum, an old oak grove, and a cemetery on the higher ground which has not been used since it was closed down in 1934. The abandoned, overgrown estate was gradually developed as clearing work advanced varying the planned scheme according to the parts newly laid bare. The task of transforming such a unique setting into a public park called for a respectful treatment of the existing elements: tumble-down walls, ruins, paths, tombs and, above all, stone and water. Old convent documents revealed that this area was the source of old fountains and washing places in the north of the city.

Álvaro Siza

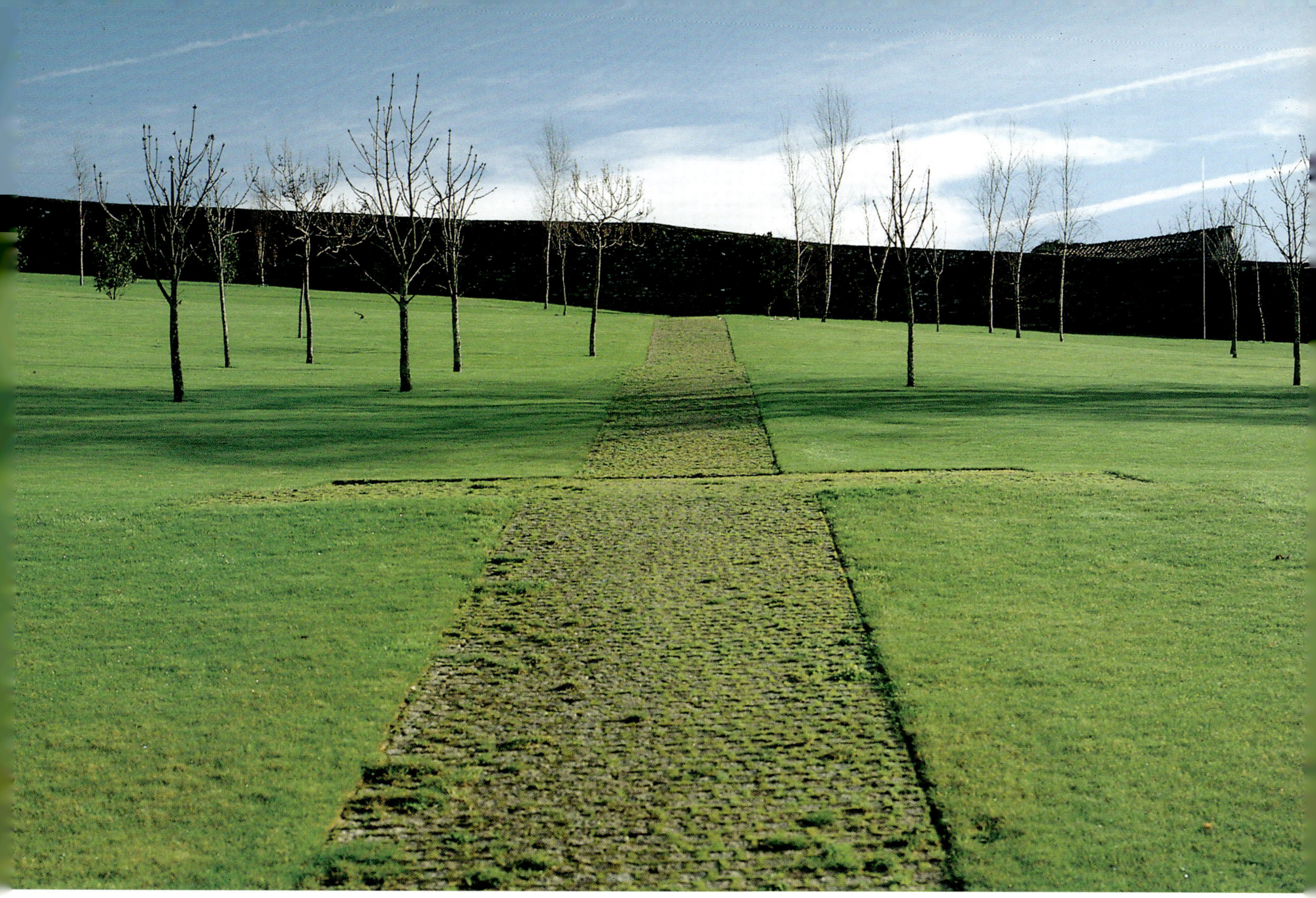

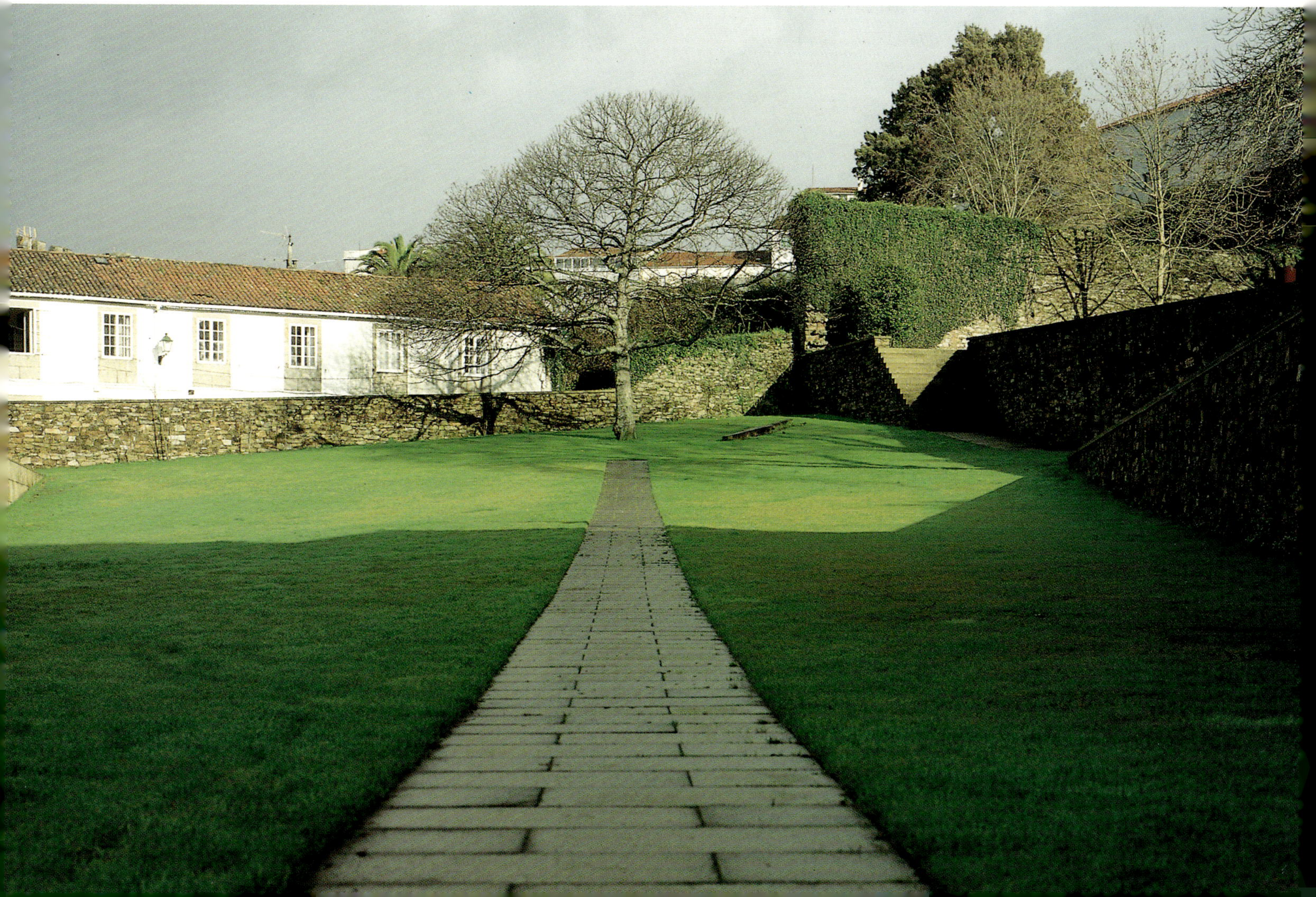

1. Housing in Oporto
1995

2. University of Aveiro
1995

3. Santa Maria de Moura Inn.
1997

*Bom Jesus House
1994*

Thanks to his academic and professional training, Souto de Moura has always been related to two famous names on the Portuguese scene: Fernando Távora, under whom he studied, and Álvaro Siza, with whom he worked for many years. His architecture, like Siza's, is based on the posits of rationalism, but in his works he tends, above all, to investigate space and how to break it down. This makes his buildings more abstract, more austere in their use of language; normally the program is comprised in a single container, though in some cases it is subject to a breaking down process. Materials are exploited to their limits to maintain an individuality which eliminates the mediating resource of the joints, thereby making the most of their expressive qualities. A similar treatment is given to other elements of the project, as in the case of the walls suspended over the ground in the Oporto Cultural Center.

Eduardo Souto de Moura (1952) graduated in 1980 from the School of Fine Arts of Oporto. From 1974 to 1979, while he was still a student, he worked in the office of Álvaro Siza. He was already building his first projects when he qualified: the recuperation of a ruin in Gerés, and the Municipal Market in Braga (1980-1984) with its two characteristic parallel walls, which are echoed in the Oporto Cultural Center (1981-1988); the facade of the Burgo project in Oporto (1991) is perhaps the most paradigmatic example of his particular use of materials. He has made his mark in the field of family houses, the most prominent of which are recent works such as the house in Tavira (Algarve, Portugal, 1991-1994), where he experimented with the articulations, and the house in Modelo (Caminha, Portugal, 1991-1997), where the only volumetric study is the roof which has "fallen from the skies", establishing a direct relationship with the place. In larger-scale commissions he continues to work with single volumes whose roofs still display the necessary fragmentation of other design elements, such as the air-conditioning units; one example of this is the Faculty of Geological Sciences in Aveiro (1990-1994). Geometric rigor continues its high profile in more recent buildings such as the residential building in Oporto (1996) and the 1993 project which is currently being constructed in Matosinhos (Portugal).

Bom Jesus House

- Location: Braga, Portugal.
- Construction: 1994.
- Architect: Eduardo Souto de Moura.
- Photographs: Lluís Ferreira Alves.

The simplicity of concept and language used in Bom Jesus House on the outskirts of Braga is a clear example of how to respond appropriately but simply and subtly to a given context, a tradition of native culture and craft, and a series of pragmatic demands.
The composition of this single-family house combines two volumes, each representing different programs and construction systems.

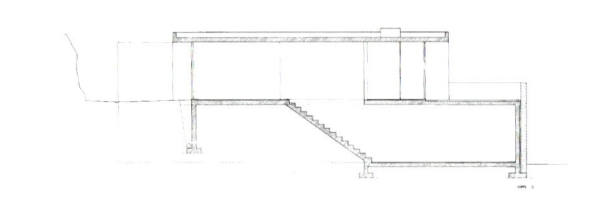

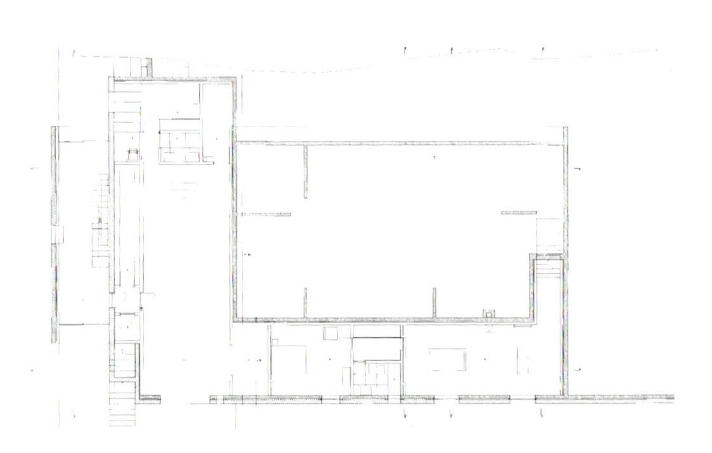

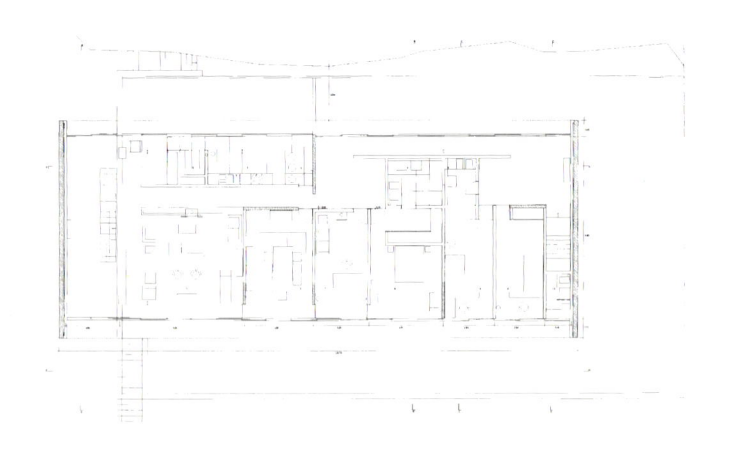

178 *Eduardo Souto de Moura*

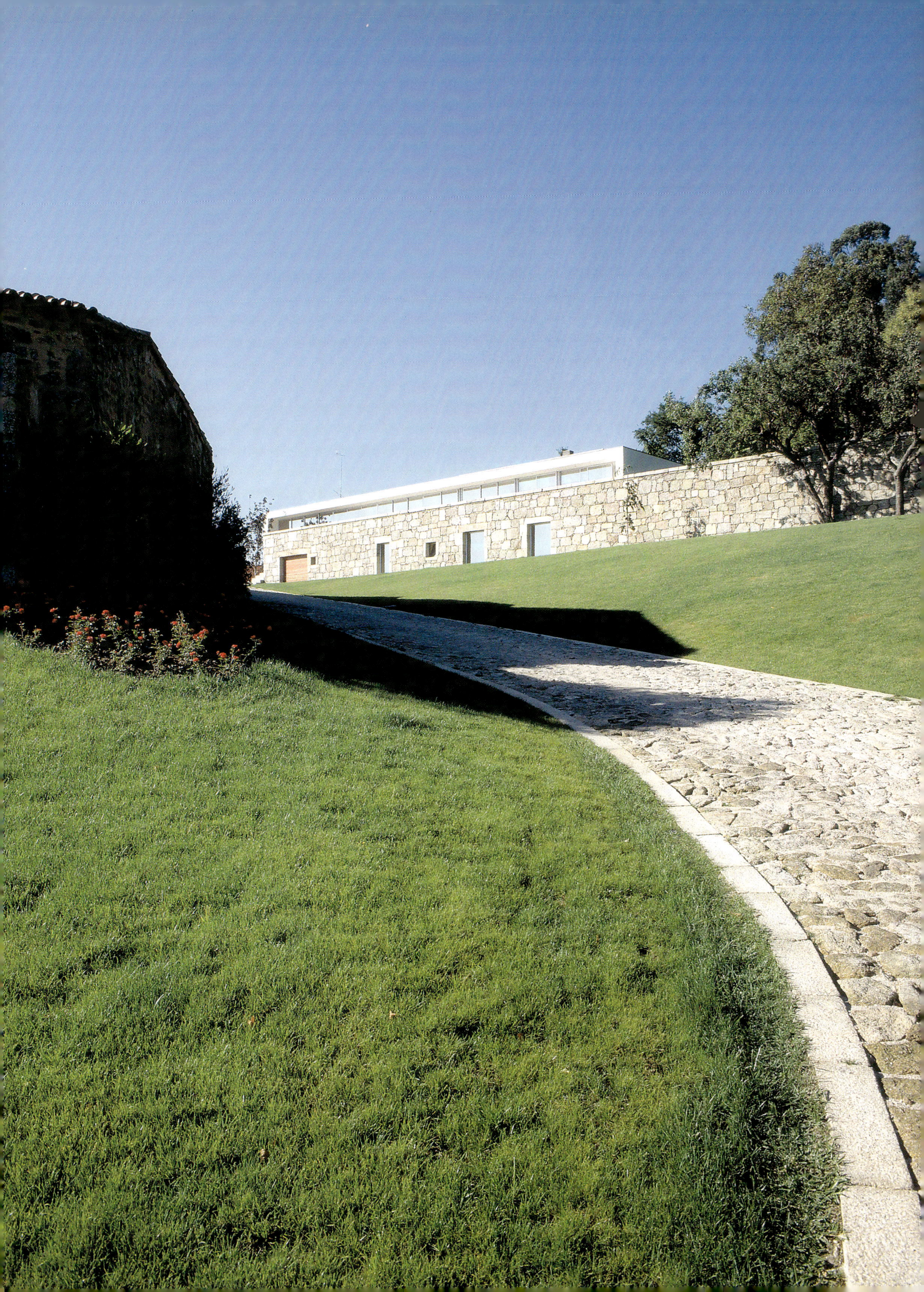

Ben van Berkel

1. Wilbrink Villa
   1994

2. Shopping Mall in Emmen
   1996

Renovation and Extension of the Twenthe National Museum 1996

The planning method used by this Dutch architect, who works in association with Caroline Bos since 1988, is based on abstract concepts represented by diagrams which study the various pressures affecting the project, ranging from the conditioning factors of the place to technology. He attempts to reflect this union of forces in movement either in the lines of the facade or in the formal image of the whole. To do this, he has recourse to asymmetry, variation of materials, and transparencies which allow us to perceive the conceptual dynamics behind them. In spite of a degree of formalism, his projects take great strength from the context, due to his purity in the treatement of volumes; reinforced by his use of materials and, in some cases, the hermetic nature of his facades. Howerer, his work also delves into complex structural techniques, generally based on digital calculation systems, as in the case of Karbouw (1990), where the geometry of the roof is resolved by means of information technology.

Ben van Berkel (1957) studied at the Rietveld Academie in Amsterdam and the Architectural Association in London, qualifying in 1987. In 1988, he set up his own studio in association with Caroline Bos (1959). One of his first projects was the Karbouw office block (Amersfoort, Holland, 1990-1992), which saw the start of his experimentation with computing applications. In 1992, he designed the self-absorbed volume of the Nijkerk Business Center (Holland), where it is impossible to find a single conventional reference to the common realm of imagery. One of his purest works in terms of volume is the REMU 50/10 KV electrical power station (Amersfoort, Holland, 1989-1993); the building is almost hermetically closed in, as all it houses are three huge transformers. His major urban interventions include Erasmus Bridge in Rotterdam (1990-1996), with an asymmetry which aims to reflect every aspect (public, urban, constructional, and architectural) of the planning process. Another outstanding intervention was the Piet Hein Tunnel (Amsterdam, 1990-1996). Particularly worthy of mention among his projects outside Holland are Yokohoma Port International Terminus (Japan, 1995) and the Boxhalle (Berlin, 1992).

Renovation and Extension of the Twenthe National Museum

- **Location:** Lasondersingel 129-131, Enschede, Holland.
- **Construction:** 1996.
- **Client:** Rijksgebouwendienst, Projects Direction (The Hague).
- **Architect:** Ben van Berkel.
- **Associates:** Harrie Pappot (project coordinator),
    Oost Hovenier (project director),
    Lodewijk Baljon (landscape architect).
- **Photographs:** Christian Richters.

The program centered on covering the rear patio, with a view to turning it into a new museum of modern art, plus the construction of a feature to connect the museum with the rear courtyard. Ben van Berkel decided to build a completely new ambience, to break with the previous image of the galleries by thoroughly treating their six inner faces. The first step was to make the most of the daylight. The translucent glass channels overhead light into the gallery, diffusing it regularly and making it slightly less direct.

Ben van Berkel

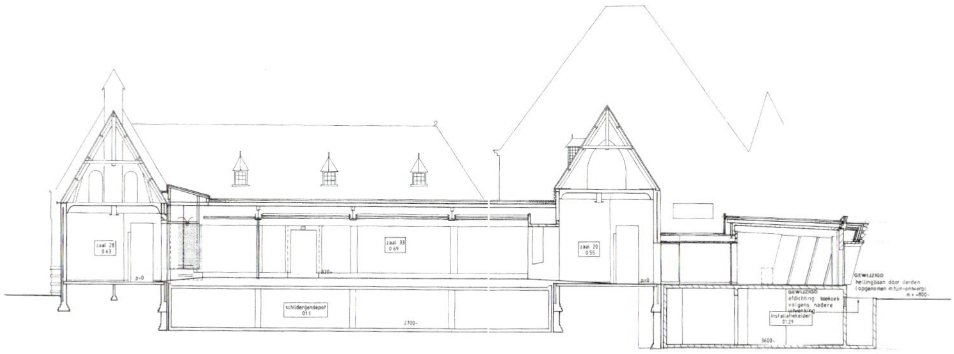

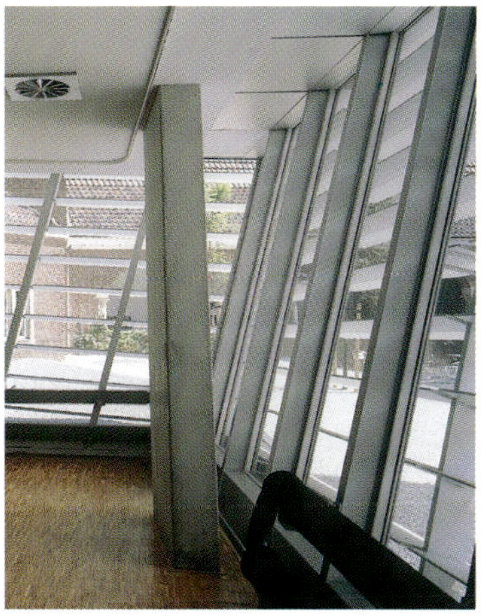

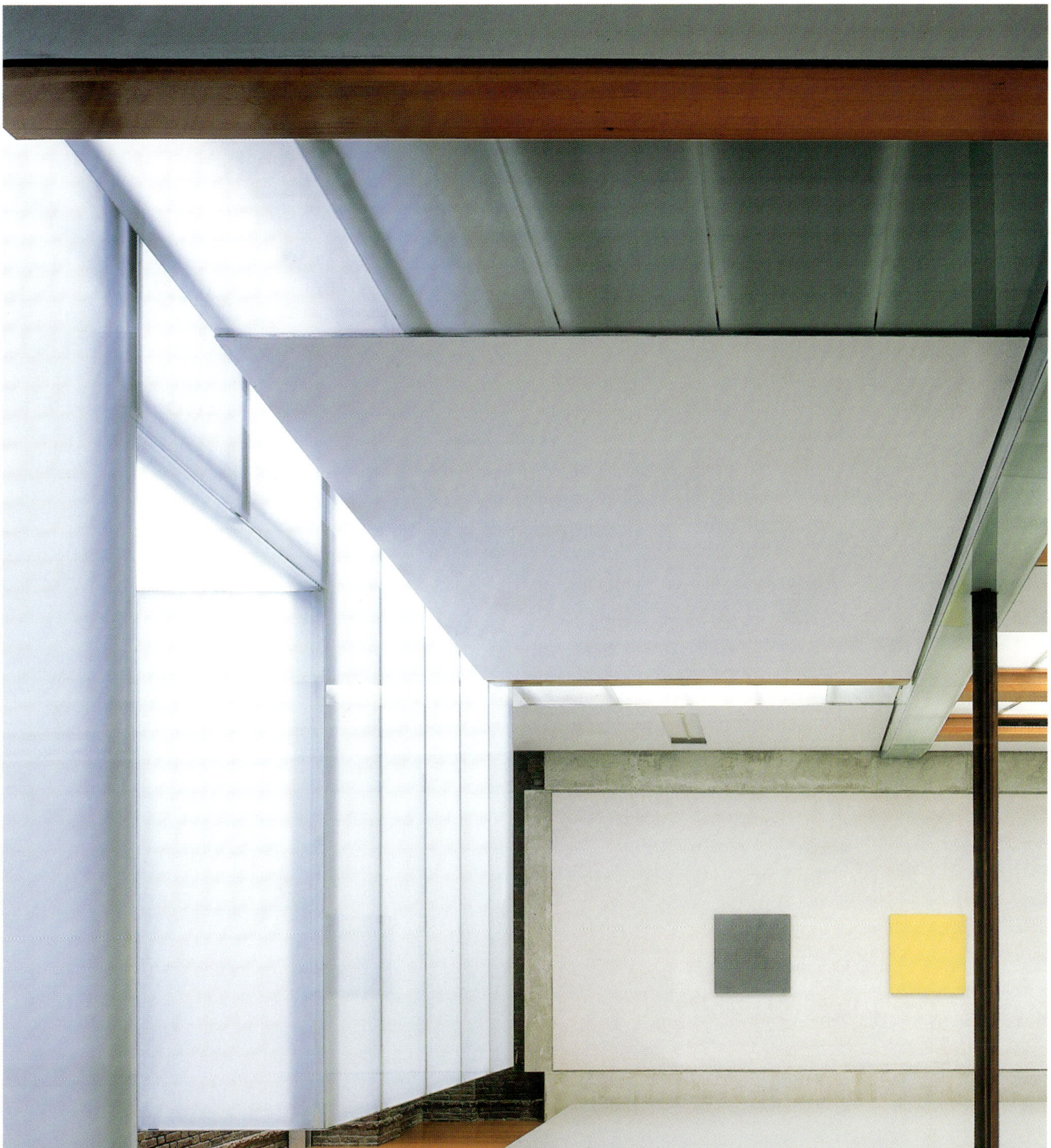

Erick van Egeraat

1. ING Bank
   1995

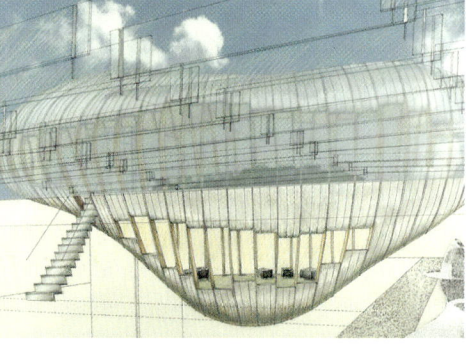

2. Secondary school in Utrecht
   1997

Van Egeraat's architecture continues to demonstrate the postulates of Mecanoo, though his new solo career strives to be much more "present-day". His architectural experience started in his student days, when he still conceived his projects as part of a Teutonic tradition, with simple but forceful ideas. His ideas have gradually moved toward cultural crosses and even being in vogue: his buildings are now much more daring, with increasingly contrasting and innovative proposals, and the ING Bank project in Budapest is a good representative of this phase. In his works, the simultaneous use of architectonic codes produces different forms of expression to produce what he calls his "Modern Baroque" phase. The detail which characterizes his earlier work – remember his studio-house in Rotterdam or his "green homes" – continues to constitute a landmark in his career. Today his architecture displays a "modishness" in that he evidently pays attention to what is going on around him and endeavors to convey what he sees to his work.

■ *Natural History Museum, Rotterdam*
1995

Erick van Egeraat (Amsterdam, 1956) studied at the University of Delft, graduating in 1984. In 1980 he set up the Mecanoo team along with Francine Houben, Hen Döll and Chris de Weijer. In 1995, he left Mecanoo to set up his own firm, EEA (Erick van Egeraat associated architects). His joint experience with Mecanoo produced one of his most prominent projects, the headquarters of National Nederlanden and the ING Bank branch in Budapest (1992-1994). Even when he was part of the team, Van Egeraat sometimes worked alone, as in the case of the 26 homes in Nimega (Netherlands, 1989-1993), which display the same design principles as those employed by the group. His various projects are marked by the simultaneous use of architectural codes applied in completely different yet contemporary ways; two examples are the great transparent parallelepiped of Ichthus College in Rotterdam (1996-1999) and the Budapest National Theater (1997), which presents the image of a great ameba flanked by glass surfaces.

Natural History Museum, Rotterdam

- **Location:** Rotterdam, Holland.
- **Construction:** 1995.
- **Architect:** Erick van Egeraat.
- **Associates:** Francine Houben, Birgit Jürgenahake, Jeroen Shipper.
- **Photographs:** Christian Richters.

The old Dijkzigt Villa, constructed in 1851 by E.L. Metzelaar, which housed the Natural History Museum, had become too small. Almost all the rooms were taken up by offices, workshops and collection storage. When an initiative emerged to restore the old villa, it was decided to build an annex to correct the museum's space problems.

The annex is designed as a counterpoint to the original villa. The materials, technology and form are absolutely different to the main body of the museum. According to Van Egeraat, the facade is conceived as the sum of three different skins. The first is concrete and encloses an exhibition room; the second is glass, like a membrane around the concrete body, though the latter penetrates it at given points to form the foyer or windows, and the third skin is built in brick.

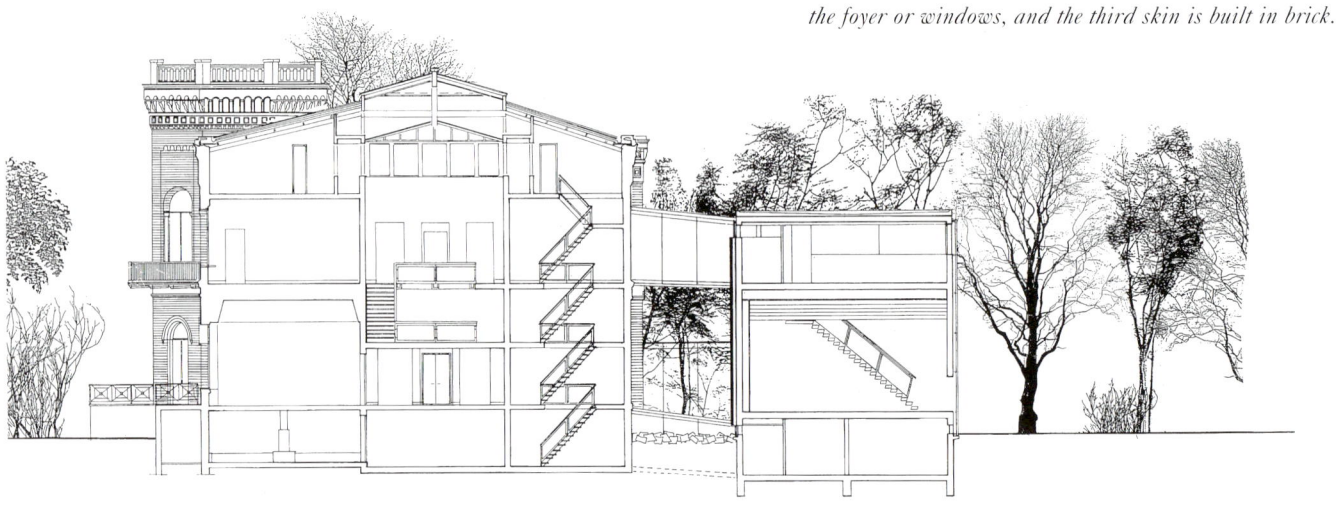

Erick van Egeraat

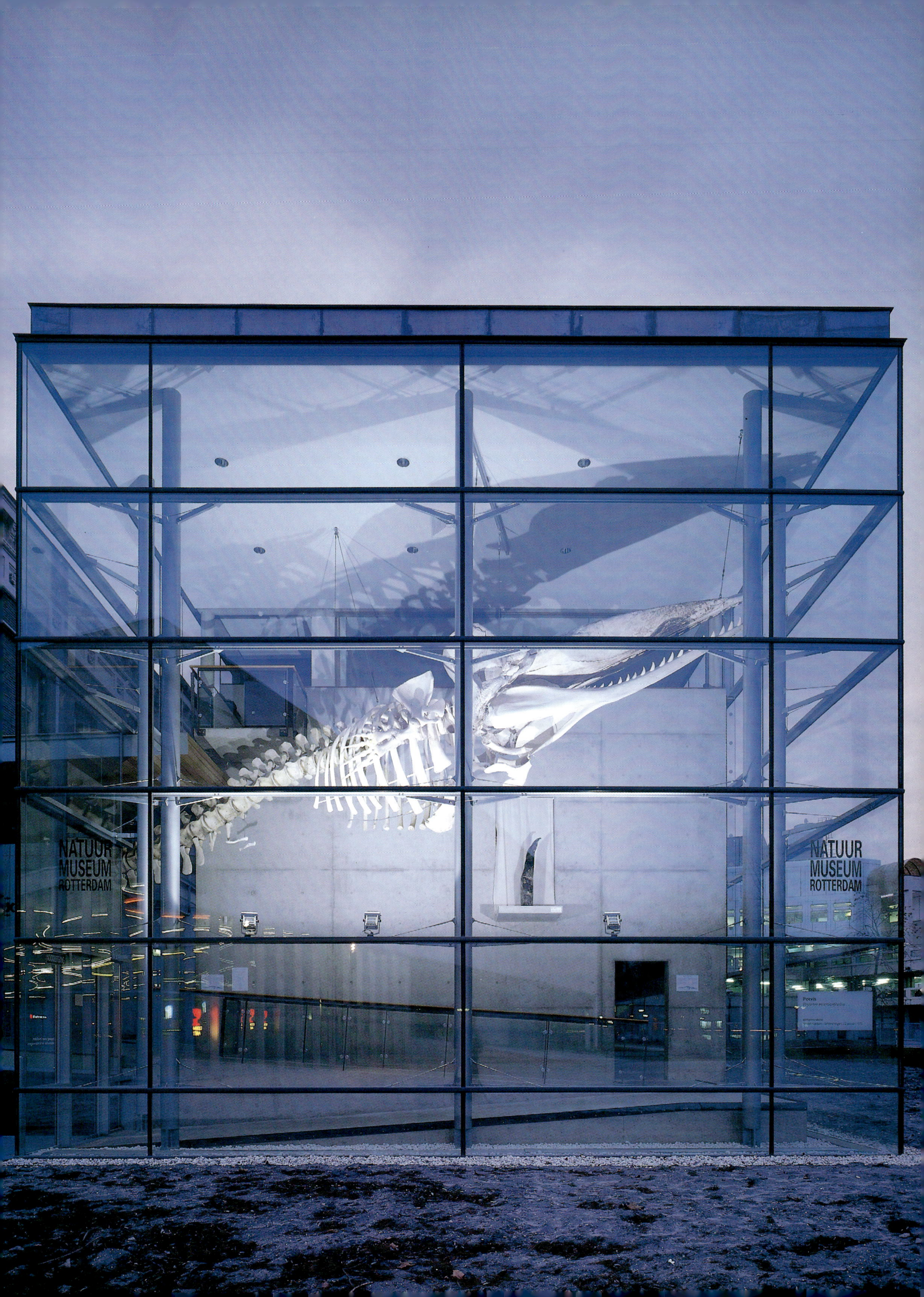
NATUUR MUSEUM ROTTERDAM
NATUUR MUSEUM ROTTERDAM

Von Gerkan + Marg

1. Bielefeld Subway Station
   1991

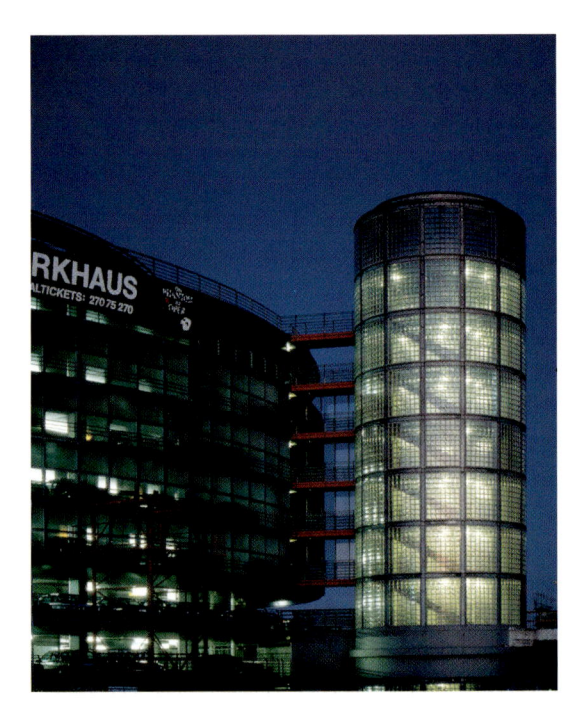

2. Hamburg Airport
   1993

3. Stuttgart Airport
   1992

*Exhibition Center in Leipzig
1997*

The career of these German designers has, for the most part, taken the form of large-scale buildings with heavy flows of visitors, such as airports, stations, parking lots, or trade fair concourses. Their buildings are large containers, where the role of technology is one of the main design factors. Their structural language tends to be clear and simple, in some cases exploring the relationship between the structures and nature, as in the case of the "trees" at Stuttgart Airport. The lightness of their structures is the product of studying the structural capacities of the materials and their combinations as bearing or enclosing elements. In their projects, they study new possibilities for roofs, such as domes and arches, along with the introduction of new materials such as glass or metal structures, which ultimately give their buildings large-scale spaces for traffic, whether air or land-bound.

Meinhard von Gerkan (1935) and Volkwin Marg (1936) studied at the Braunschweig Technical University and graduated in 1964. In 1965, they embarked on their professional practice as partners. One of their first large-scale structures was Tegel Airport in Berlin (1965-1975), planned on the basis of a hexagonal geometric design. This was followed by many airport design competitions: Munich (1975), Moscow (1976), also built on a hexagonal basis, Dar el Beida in Algeria (1976), Pyongyang (1985-1986), Paderborn (1989), Cologne (1989), City Schönefeld in Berlin (1994), and Zurich (1996). In 1980, they won the competition to design Stuttgart Airport, which was constructed between 1991 and 1993, and in 1986, the competition for Hamburg Airport, which was built in 1993. They have also designed train stations, such as Stuttgart 21 (1994), where they continue to experiment with curved structures, and the great domes of Frankfurt 21 (1996). Turning to design for "motorized traffic", they designed the parking lot for the Hillmann in Bremen (1983-1984) and the great cylinder of the parking lot at Hamburg Airport (1990). In 1996, they designed the glass dome of the Leipzig Exhibition Center. This project highlights the team's structural maturity covering the points which anchor the glass and the self-bearing dome structure.

Exhibition Center in Leipzig

- Location: Messeallee, 1, Leipzig, Germany.
- Date of construction: 1997.
- Architect: Von Gerkam, Marg & Partner.
- Structures: Ian Ritchie Architects, London.
- Landscape architects: Wehberg, Eppinger, Schmidtke.
- Photographs: Busam/Richter Architekturphoto.

One of the keys to the development of the complex was separating the circulation into two different levels. The lower, ground-level floor provides for the reception, orientation, and distribution of visitors, while the upper floor leads into exhibition and meeting spaces. By increasing the density of construction, distances were kept short, all for the convenience of the user. At all points, the supports of the glass skin are anchored from the outside, leaving the glass to shine in all its tautness on the inside, free of obstacles.

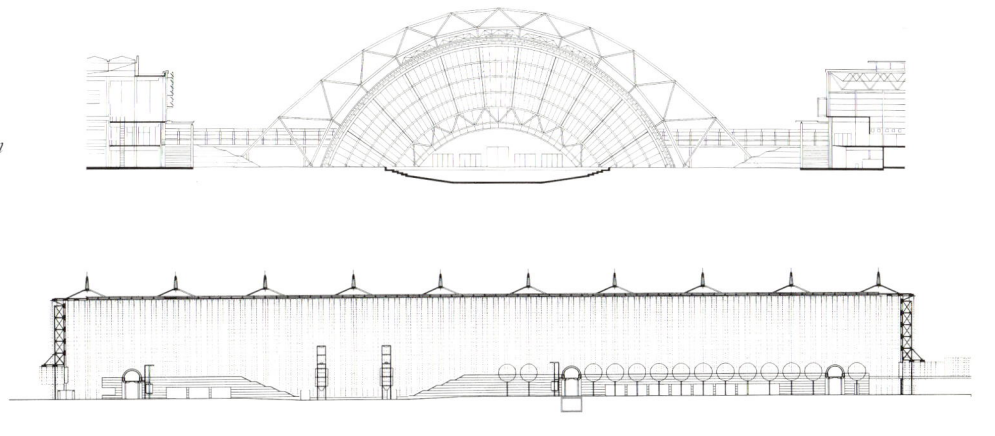

Exhibition Center in Leipzig 191